BIBLICAL PERSPECTIVES ON EVANGELISM

LIVING IN A THREE-STORIED UNIVERSE

Walter Brueggemann

ABINGDON PRESS
Nashville

BIBLICAL PERSPECTIVES ON EVANGELISM:
LIVING IN A THREE-STORIED UNIVERSE

Copyright © 1993 by Abingdon Press

98   99   00   01   02 — 11   10   9   8   7

Library of Congress Cataloging-in-Publication Data

Brueggemann, Walter.
 Biblical perspectives on evangelism: living in a three-storied universe /
Walter Brueggemann.
  p. cm.
 Includes bibliographical references
 ISBN 0-687-41233-1 (pbk. : alk. paper)
 1. Evangelistic work—Biblical teaching.   I. Title
BS680.E86B78   1993   93-10804
269'.2—dc20   CIP

BIBLICAL PERSPECTIVES ON EVANGELISM

CONTENTS

INTRODUCTION

Evangelism is currently a passionate preoccupation of the U.S. church. This accent on evangelism is no doubt a reflection of the deep crisis facing the church. On the surface, there is a "drive for survival" as mainline churches notice diminished membership, diminished dollars, and eroding influence and importance. Below that surface agenda, there is the growing awareness among us of the resistance of our culture to the primary claims of the gospel. That resistance takes the form of secularism, ofttimes expressed as indifference, and frequently evokes in response a kind of fearful legalism. It is clear, however, that the power of secularism is finally destructive, and that the reaction of legalism provides no adequate response or resolve on the part of the church. Beneath the growing awareness of that hostility to the gospel, moreover, there is the simple "news" of the gospel itself that provides a missionary impetus for sharing the news with our "news starved" society. Finally the ground of evangelism is found in the gospel itself, and not in any church condition or societal need. The urgency of evangelism thus is a multilayered and complex reality in the church. For that reason, it does not surprise us that there is no ready agreement among us on the meaning of evangelism, let alone consensus about strategies and procedures. Indeed, evangelism clearly means many different things to many different people.

For that reason, it is not surprising that evangelism, to a scripture teacher, in large part consists of attending to and participating in the transformational drama that is enacted in the biblical text itself. In what follows, I argue that the decisive clues for our practice of evangelism are found in the drama and dynamic transaction of the biblical text itself. This claim requires on our part a very different understanding of and relation to the text. In what follows, I assume that the biblical text is not a handbook for morality or doctrine as it is often regarded, nor on the other hand, is it an historical record, as many are wont to take it. Rather the biblical text is the articulation of imaginative models of reality in which "text-users," i.e., readers in church and synagogue, are invited to participate. The texts continue to be alive and invitational because they refuse to stay "back there," but always insist upon being "present tense" and contemporary. Thus biblical texts were not simply formed and fixed (either by some once-for-all divine disclosure or by some nameable human author); they were shaped by and for repeated use in the community, especially in the practice of worship, but in many other contexts as well.

And when the community of faith "uses" a text in its own life and practice, it reenacts not only the substantive (moral, doctrinal) claims of the text, but also the dramatic, transformational potential of the text. Thus I propose that such a dramatic, dynamic understanding of the biblical text as imaginative model of reality provides an important interface with the church's current preoccupation with evangelism.

Evangelism, I propose, is "doing the text" again, as our text and as "news" addressed to us and waiting to be received, appropriated, and enacted in our own time and place. By "doing the text," I mean to entertain, attend to, participate in, and reenact the drama of the text. To be sure, not all texts are for us useable models, depending upon our understanding of the gospel. And not all texts have equal transformative potential. In what follows, I have obviously selected texts which make a certain kind of presentation from a certain angle about the "news." I have no doubt that some trajectories of texts are peculiarly pertinent to our theme of evangelism and our moment of faithfulness in the life of the church, and so I have stacked the cards in that direction. In doing so, I appeal especially to the practice of Luther and Calvin who focused on texts which voiced the gospel.

It is my judgment that in the fraudulent and counter-productive quarrels in the church between "liberals" and "conservatives," the dramatic power of the text has largely been lost. In its place has come either the liberal misreading toward "expressive individualism" or the conservative propensity toward legalistic conformity which in the end is characteristically allied with free market politics and economics. In such a situation as ours, I propose, evangelism begins in the church's emancipation from "expressive individualism" and/or legalistic conformity, and a reembrace of the textual drama whereby this community has recurrently embraced new life that touches every dimension of its existence. The biblical text has a voice of its own, other than ours. "Doing the text" means letting the voice of the text have its full say in our common life.

In speaking of a "three-storied universe," my title is intended to be a helpful and suggestive play on words. On the one hand, the phrase alludes to the highly influential and disputed work of Rudolf Bultmann, a great and important New Testament scholar of the last generation. Bultmann observed that the Bible, living in the world of ancient science and myth, assumed that the universe was three storied or three tiered, with the earth as the second story, the heavens above as the top story and the waters beneath as the bottom floor. This view of the universe was not deliberately thought through in the Bible, but was readily and uncritically appropriated as an established cultural, liturgical, and scientific assumption.

The play on words which I intend, on the other hand, recognizes that the word "story" can refer to "floors" or "tiers" in an architectural arrangement. But the same term can of, course, refer to narratives. My use of the phrase three-storied universe alludes to Bultmann, but means to suggest that the Bible revolves around three narratives which are focal and normative, which drive the imagination of Israel, and which generate many derivative claims. These three stories are the *promise* made to the ancestors, the *deliverance* from slavery, and the gift of the *land*. These three stories are definitional for Israel's self-understanding, and provide much of the material for Christian proclamation, done with great interpretive freedom. It is my argument that evangelism means inviting people into these stories as the definitional story of our life, and thereby authorizing people to give up, abandon, and renounce other stories that have shaped their lives in false or distorting ways.

The three-storied universe of the Bible is indeed an odd world which makes no accommodation to the epistemology of the modern world. I suggest, however, no support for demythologization of that odd universe. Bultmann proposes that one must transpose these ancient narratives into more palatable modern accounts of reality, because they are cast in such pre-scientific, pre-modern modes. Against such an "emptying" of the stories which Bultmann then "refills" with modern categories, I propose the stories must be kept in their embarrassing ancientness, for along with the refusal of modernity comes God as a vital and key character in this account of our lives. It is not, so it seems, possible to modernize the narratives without losing the primitiveness of this character who must be kept as the focal point of "the news." The ancient stories of the Bible are indeed sense-making midst our pervasive "non-sense."

Thus evangelism, as it "does the text" in our time and place, insists that this account of lived reality is more adequate than rival accounts that are given us in the alternatives of secularism and legalism that are all around us. Evangelism, I propose, is the invitation to reimagine our lives in these narrative modes. The hearing of these narratives of reality makes us more inescapably aware that an attempt to live without the Holy Character of these narratives is indeed a life of "non-sense." (To be sure, one outside the story will not find such a judgment persuasive, but the nerve of evangelism depends upon such a contrast.)

The oddness of the biblical world and its rationality (and its notion of three stories) are not defined by archaic physics or modern scientific models of reality. My understanding of evangelism as entry into the "three stories" invites us to re-experience and relive our lives according to *the promise* to the ancestors, *the liberation* of slaves, and *the gift of land* to displaced peasants. These three stories contain poignant good news about God, the promise-maker, the liberator, the promise-keeper, the one who is alive and available only in the mediations of these narratives. Thus I propose that evangelism is indeed to do again and again what Jews and Christians have always done, to tell "the old, old story," but to do so in ways that impact every aspect of our contemporary life, public and personal. The stories themselves are vehicles whereby all things are made new.

Those who come to hear these stories (and those who tell them) do not come to "the meeting" "story-less," as though we are void of other stories. Rather we come with our imagination already saturated with other stories to which we have already made trusting (even if unwitting) commitment. These other stories may be derived from various ideologies that reflect dominant values in our culture. By their constant retelling (through propaganda and advertising, or even through parental inculcation), we have come to take these other stories for granted and as "given."

In the matrix of evangelism, we are prepared to notice that these stories we have embraced without great intentionality are not adequate. They have severe limitations and cannot generate the life for which we yearn. The reason they are less than adequate stories is that they lack the life-giving power of holiness out beyond our selves to which we must have access if we are to live fully human lives. Thus the enactment of the narratives of the biblical text provides an alternative reality. On the one hand, this alternative voicing of reality makes available to us the terrible, life-giving reality of God. On the other hand, these stories with their core character permit us to notice the shallowness of the stories we have embraced from elsewhere. The telling and hearing of this "three-storied reality" is an invitation and summons to "switch stories," and therefore to change lives. The telling and hearing constitute a wrenching encounter that leaves nothing of "business as usual," as it did not for the ancient users of these stories. The wonder is that these old texts as models of alternative imagination do indeed continue to have that generative, transformative capacity, even in our time and place.

The plan of this book is divided into two parts. In the first quite extended chapter, I have proposed a "taxonomy of evangelism." That is, I have identified what I take to be the recurring elements and sequence of the enactment of the "good news," as it is enacted in the texts themselves. I mean to suggest that there is no single narrative in the Bible that is the normative account of the "news" (even as the early church leaves us with four Gospel accounts, and not one single normative one). Rather there are characteristic re-tellings that take a variety of forms, told with constancy, but with considerable imagination and flexibility. Our own entry into and participation in this grid of re-telling invites us to the same imagination and flexibility, but always with the same characteristic elements and sequences.

The second part of the book (chapters 2 through 4) takes up "meetings" wherein the news of *promise* to the ancestors in Genesis, *liberation* in the book of Exodus, and *land* in the book of Joshua becomes the subject of discussion. I judge that these narratives, told in many forms, tell the truth of our lives, both the truth about our most element needs, and the truth about God's most faithful gifts that make human life possible.

I have imagined that these definitional stories are offered in a "meeting" where the news is announced and received. In chapter 2, I consider the meeting with Joshua in Joshua 24 whereby *an outsider* is included as an insider in these element narratives. In chapter 3, *a jaded, forgetful insider* is brought to the meeting with Ezra in Nehemiah 8, and in the meeting is invited back into the memory that gives life. In chapter 4, I take up a third constituency for evangelism, namely *the young of the believing community*, i.e., children of believers. But here a different approach is required, because with the young, an ongoing conversation replaces a single, identifiable meeting.

Thus my argument is that *outsiders, jaded insiders,* and *children-becoming-adults* are primary constituencies for evangelism. In each case, I suggest, there is a powerful and poignant interface between text and folk. And when the text is well said and well heard, folk are brought to wondrous "news."

This book has come about for me because of the church's crisis around the issue of evangelism. The first chapter had its origin as a paper which I presented at an evangelism conference in Charlotte, N.C., sponsored by Columbia Theological Seminary, Princeton Theological Seminary, and Union Theological Seminary (Richmond). It is reprinted here, with minor revisions, by the kind permission of CTS Press, which first printed the papers from the conference (*Evangelism in the Reformed Tradition,* edited by Arnold B. Lowell, 1990). The other chapters began life as papers presented to my own church, the United Church of Christ, in a series of Institutes on Evangelism. In that context, I am grateful for the hospitality of Alan Johnson, Robert Sandman, and Roger Knight.

As is usual for me, I am grateful to Tempie Alexander and Donna Lograsso for their patient expertise in typing the manuscript. My final thanks is to my colleague Ben Johnson, whose generosity and graciousness have made it possible for me to dare to comment on the vexed and urgent subject of evangelism. It is clear, in the end, that evangelism cannot be a program strategy, but a revolutionary way of enacting the hope and energy of the believing community. I am grateful that my work not only can be addressed to that community, but comes from my life in it.

All scriptural quotations and chapter and verse references are from the New Revised Standard Version of the Bible, with one exception. The divine name, YHWH in Hebrew, is traditionally rendered "LORD" in most English translations, including the NRSV. I have preferred to use "YHWH" or "Yahweh."

Walter Brueggemann
Columbia Theological Seminary
January 8, 1993

CHAPTER 1

Evangelism in Three Unfinished Scenes

For all our confusion and disagreement about the meaning of evangelism, it is important to identify, as best we can, the structure, sequence, and elements of the "news event," in the Bible itself. I shall argue in this chapter that acts of evangelism have a characteristic structure and recurring pattern which are worth noticing. That structure and pattern are in part shaped by *the material claim* that "God has triumphed," a claim made repeatedly in various ways. But the structure and pattern are also part of a determined *rhetorical intentionality*. This is the way in which the community within these texts speaks about what is most crucial and transformative in its life and identity. The *material claim* can never be separated from *rhetorical intentionality*. Part of the task concerning evangelism is to recover nerve about our modes of speech in church traditions that have debased our speech, either by conservative reductionism or by liberal embarrassment.

The noun "gospel," which means "message," is linked in the Bible to the verb "tell-the-news" (one word, *bissar*, in Hebrew). At the center of the act of evangelism is the message announced, a verbal, out-loud assertion of something decisive not known until this moment of utterance. There is no way that anyone, including an embarrassed liberal, can avoid this lean, decisive assertion which is at the core of evangelism.

14

The act of announcement, however, is not barren and context-less. I argue here that the announcement itself is the middle term of a three-part dramatic sequence. No reductionist conservative can faithfully treat evangelism as though it were only "naming the name." We are required to notice that behind (prior to) the announcement is an "event" of mythic proportion to which we have no direct access. And after the proclamation comes the difficult, demanding work of reordering all of life according to the claim of the proclaimed verdict.

It is clear then, that the taxonomy I suggest here concerning evangelism intends to critique and reject many popular notions of evangelism. The reader is urged not to assume that this taxonomy will accommodate many of our careless and ill-thought notions and practices of evangelism. This way of understanding evangelism is a challenge to the *epistemology* of many culture-accommodating Christians. Conversely it is a challenge as well to the *ecclesial, economic* practice of Christians who have spiritualized and privatized the gospel away from its demanding social, this-worldly dimension.

◆　　◆　　◆

The parable was enacted in St. Louis about a decade ago. The then St. Louis football Cardinals were playing the much despised Washington Redskins, coached by the wondrously hated George Allen. As the clock ran out, with the Redskins leading by less than six points, the Cardinals made their last play. Jim Hart threw a pass to Mel Gray in the end-zone. The ball settled into Gray's hands, and through, and on to the turf. One official signaled a touchdown that gave the Cardinals a victory. An official on the other side of the end-zone signaled an incomplete, dropped pass, and thus a defeat. It could not be both ways. The two officials saw it differently.

It was a disputed call on which much was at stake, a lot of money, some reputations, pride, a different future. The six officials huddled at mid-field. It was like a meeting of the gods, "fixing the destinies" of the earth. The packed stadium was very quiet, for over five minutes. "How silently, how silently, the wondrous gift is given." Even the radio announcers stopped their chatter. Then, in a moment of epiphany, perhaps conceding home-field advantage and bias, the referee raised his hands — a completed pass for the Cardinals, a touchdown, a victory! The Cardinals had won, the despised Redskins were defeated, and the hated George Allen was given his just deserts. This really is a moral universe! You know, do you not, that the stadium and the media and the city went wild. (Nobody at that time was moving the Cardinals to Phoenix.)

Of course, I was not at the game. I saw none of the action. I only stayed glued to the radio. I saw none of it in person. I relied completely on the trustworthiness of Jack Buck and the other announcers whom I had learned to trust. I listened to and loved their over-stated, imaginative rendering and reconstruction of the drama of the game. I took them at their word, believed them, and knew for sure what had happened. I learned second hand, but it was good enough for me.

It was only a football game at second hand; for that day, however, it was a transformative event. I promptly phoned my son to be sure he knew. I treated myself to extra popcorn, and I went to my study, vindicated, energized, convinced that all was right in the world. I was indeed pleased to be living in such a triumphant place as St. Louis. Many others, both in St. Louis and in Washington, were getting used to the new reality that was variously good news and bad news.

You will forgive such a partisan and commonplace tale. I tell it because it offers all the ingredients of the drama of salvation. I propose that the signal of a touchdown was something like an "evangelical" announcement. That "event" provides a way to identify the ingredients that belong to such news.

THE DRAMA IN THREE SCENES

Evangelism is a *drama*, a narrative account that has a beginning, a middle, and an end. It is not an isolated event or simply a decision. It is a process that has many characters. For the drama to work properly, each character must play a proper role.

This drama, in its narrative shape, has *three scenes*. In the first scene, there is combat, struggle, and *conflict between powerful forces* who battle for control of the turf, control of the payoffs, control of the future. Evangelism makes no sense unless the drama is understood *agonistically*, i.e., as combat and struggle. In my tale, the combat concerned the Cardinals and the Redskins, George Allen and one of the many, constantly changing Cardinal coaches. I myself was not even present to the event that mattered most. In this first scene, there is not only struggle, but there are third-party voices (the officials) who render a clean and decisive verdict about the data which itself may be ambiguous. One cannot report that the pass was thrown, perhaps dropped, perhaps held. There must be an adjudication that overrides the ambiguity and makes the outcome clear. So the stadium is filled with silent waiting, until the judges flash their verdicts. When the scores are given, then, only then do we know.

In the second scene, there is an additional character not present in the first scene. It is the announcer, the proclaimer, *the witness who gives testimony and tells the outcome he has watched.* If you have listened to any of these football announcers, it will not bother you when they speak in stylized clichés, for all the announcers speak in clichés. The purpose of the announcer is to make the outcome available, credible, significant, and present tense to those who were not there and who saw nothing, but who receive what happened at second hand. (My image of myself is as a young boy, crowded with the family around the radio at night, hearing the shrieking voice of Harry Cary, projecting over the static, so that the outcome of Cardinal baseball mattered in Blackburn, Missouri, as much as it mattered in St. Louis.)

It is of the essence of announcing, of being a messenger, of doing the work of an evangelist, that events that happened in one place matter decisively in another place, that victories won in one time continue to count decisively in another time.[1] The transferral of significance from one time to another, from one place to another, depends utterly on the effectiveness, trustworthiness, and artistic, imaginative capacity of the announcer. It is the announcer who retells, reconstructs, and reenacts for new listeners. When I heard Jack Buck that day against the Redskins, I imagined that I was present, that I had seen the pass completed, that I had watched face-to-face, with utter delight, the ritual humiliation of George Allen.

In the third scene, the announcer has now spoken and the listener has heard. The conflict is over, the announcing has ended. Now the listener must make *an appropriate response* to the new situation, letting the newly announced reality reshape life in new ways. In the football game, response to the new reality might have been collecting the office pool, or buying season tickets for next year, or taking the kids out to play football, letting Jim Hart for now be the model and fantasy for young futures.

The sequence of the drama has changed reality: the conflict is *cleanly resolved*, the conflict is *credibly announced*, the conflict is *seriously appropriated*. The news of the game has impinged upon the lives of those not present.

This drama in three scenes is *not finished*. Each scene must be endlessly reenacted. The first scene of actual conflict must always be done over again, because the Washington Redskins do not stay defeated. The victory must be re-won and reenacted each year, once in St. Louis (or now Phoenix) and once in Washington, and there is always "next year." Moreover, George Allen does not stay sufficiently hated in St. Louis. That hate must be reenacted as well. The players, coaches, fans, and announcers have long memories and grudges concerning heroes and bums, who must be "re-named" all over again. Each time over, the outcome again and again is placed in jeopardy, until the scene is completed again. Each time completed, the observers and benefactors regard this one as the real one, until it must be done again next time.

The second scene of *credible announcement* and proclamation can never be done only once. The need for replication is for two reasons. First, there are always new participants in the enterprise who were not present in the first telling, so that the event from that time and place must always again be moved to new times and places. The announcer knows that the event retold continues to be an event of transformative significance in each new retelling. The other reason for the endless retelling is that the announcers, even in the off-season of the sport, continue to retell, to find better phrases, to grasp the finer nuances, to devise better artistry, so that the primal agonistic event can be reentered and entered again, each time with more discernment and more awed mystery. What father does not want to "re-announce" to his son the events when there were "real players" of a promethean kind?

The third scene of *appropriation of the news* is never finished. The serious listener must continue to ponder, process, explore, decide, and risk to see what else this transformative news touches that was not at first evident. The ripple effect of a football victory might in the long run be changed urban economic development, the building of hotels, the scheduling of flights, and the creation of jobs. At the same time, such a victory, rightly announced, might seduce a kid's fantasy away from baseball and toward football. The announcer, in artistically announcing the outcome which in each telling is new, does not know what odd and demanding appropriations are authorized by the news. In what follows, I will explicate these three dramatic scenes, always unfinished, and then draw some conclusions for our own practice of evangelism.

THE THEOLOGICAL CONFLICT

The first scene of evangelism is a *theological conflict* hidden from our eyes, to which we have no direct access. That struggle is beyond our horizon; we have access to it only through the long narrative process of imagination, whereby we accept an agonistic rendering of cosmic reality. We have no single normative shape for the rendering to which we can make ontological appeal.[2] We have only many variant artistic tellings, none of which has logical priority:

- good vs. evil;
- life vs. death;
- Yahweh vs. Pharaoh;
- Jesus vs. Satan, sin, and death.

These oppositions are all bold attempts to portray lived reality according to a partisan set of memories, metaphors, and symbols which shape reality in a certain way. There are two matters at issue in these characteristic renderings by the community of faith. On the one hand, we do indeed want to claim a victory. Of course, the news is good news. On the other hand, however, before a victory can be claimed, we must establish the metaphor of a ground of conflict, i.e., that there really is a massive, albeit hidden, struggle for the shape, governance, and future of the world. That struggle has had some decisive turns in our favor, but it is not yet finally and fully resolved.

The Bible gives us no single event which dominates this drama of conflict and victory, but many alternative enactments and re-tellings, one as significant as another. I do not suggest that every text or all texts follow the dramatic sequence outlined here. I suggest only that this taxonomy is one predominant pattern in scripture. This patterning is important on two accounts. On the one hand, this pattern seems to recur in what are pivotal turning points in the larger text. On the other hand, these texts are the texts that the Jewish and Christian communities of interpretation characteristically treat as decisive for the theological "meat" of scripture. I readily acknowledge that there are many texts which fall outside this grid, and some which directly controvert it. In communities of faith which practice something like "canonical reading" (which I am prepared to do), it is clear that these same texts exercise paramount authority within the Bible, an authority established by use and by conviction. Thus my presentation is an act of advocacy and not of disinterested neutrality. It is an advo-cacy, I suggest, that is congruent with the practice of these communities. My sense of texts follows that rough consensus of use and conviction. Consider these several versions of the first scene, the scene of conflict in which powerful forces battle to control the future. This scene is decisive for all that follows; this scene is at the same time the most difficult for our general theme of evangelism.

One telling of this first scene is that the conflict is *a struggle among the gods*, the God of life and the powerful gods of death. Such a telling is found in the old myths behind the Bible and in the late developments of biblical apocalyptic.[3] This is the most elemental, comprehensive, and primitive telling of the first scene. There is a battle or a contest among the gods. Then there is a meeting of the gods to adjudicate the struggle, much like the football officials adjudicated at Busch Stadium. The larger gallery of the gods wait for a verdict and the outcome of the conflict.

There is a hush in heaven until the verdict is given, much like

the waiting at the Olympics after the ice skating events. Then there
is a vote given by the several gods, 9.1 for Yahweh, 9.6, 9.4, 8.9,
4.3 [Romania!], and the stands are filled with applause. In the
Israelite telling, Yahweh is declared the winner:

> For great is YHWH, and greatly to be praised;
>> he is to be revered above all gods.
> For all the gods of the peoples are idols,
>> but YHWH made the heavens.
> Honor and majesty are before him;
>> strength and beauty are in his sanctuary.
>> (Ps. 96:4-6)

The verdict is announced by the managers of the ritual; the world
is freshly entrusted to the rule of Yahweh.

A second telling of the same news from the conflict is *the Exodus
narrative.* Now the struggle invades political reality. The conflict is
between Yahweh and Pharaoh, the guarantor of freedom versus
the lord of social oppression. The combat is carried out through
the agency of Moses in the plague cycle, but Yahweh's will for
freedom is the driving power of the narrative. As one moves
through the narrative, the outcome is not clear until the very end,
until we are able to see the Egyptians dead upon the seashore
(Exod. 14:30-31). Only then do we know that the deathly power of
the empire has been overcome.

We can see from the poetry that Israel delighted to tell and to
retell this great victory with as much detail and poignancy as
possible. Moses sings:

> Pharaoh's chariots and his army he cast into the
>> sea;
>> his picked officers were sunk in the Red Sea.
> The floods covered them;
>> they went down into the depths like a stone.
> Your right hand, O YHWH, glorious in power —
>> your right hand, O YHWH, shattered the enemy.
> In the greatness of your majesty you overthrew
>> your adversaries;
>> you sent out your fury, it consumed them

> like stubble.
> At the blast of your nostrils the waters piled up,
>> the floods stood up in a heap;
>> the deeps congealed in the heart of the sea.
> The enemy said, "I will pursue, I will overtake,
>> I will divide the spoil, my desire shall have
>>> its fill of them.
>> I will draw my sword, my hand shall destroy
>>> them."
> You blew with your wind, the sea covered them;
>> they sank like lead in the mighty waters.
>> (Exod. 15:4-10)

The victory is clearly announced in the concluding doxology in which Pharaoh, empire, and injustice are completely nullified from the horizon of Israel:

> YHWH will reign forever and ever. (v. 18)

A third retelling of this basic conflict and victory is given among *the exiles in Babylon.* The oppressive power of Babylon seemed to be beyond challenge. That historical experience of exile, however, is recast by the poet into a liturgic drama of a conflict between the gods of Babylon and the power of Yahweh. Again, it is no equal contest. Yahweh enters the conflict with power and tenderness:

> See, YHWH God comes with might,
>> and his arm rules for him;
> his reward is with him,
>> and his recompense before him.
> He will feed his flock like a shepherd;
>> he will gather the lambs in his arms,
> and carry them in his bosom,
>> and gently lead the mother sheep. (Isa. 40:10-11)

Or the metaphor is changed by the poet to that of a courtroom. Yahweh takes the other gods to court and invites them to give an account of themselves. They, however, are numb, mute, and impotent:

Set forth your case, says YHWH;
    bring your proofs, says the King of Jacob.
Let them bring them, and tell us
    what is to happen.
Tell us the former things, what they are,
    so that we may consider them,
    and that we may know their outcome;
    or declare to us the things to come.
Tell us what is to come hereafter,
    that we may know that you are gods;
    do good, or do harm,
    that we may be afraid and terrified.
You, indeed, are nothing,
    and your work is nothing at all;
    whoever chooses you is an abomination.
    (Isa. 41:21-24)

The outcome of the trial in this retelling is that the power of the empire has evaporated; the authority of Yahweh is clear and unambiguous. The Lord of freedom, justice, and homecoming is on the move, for the battle is decisively ended. The other gods are driven from power; Yahweh emerges from the conflict fully established in power.

A fourth retelling is *the conflict between the deep, oppressive despair of the Roman Empire and the powerful messianic hope of Judaism*. Rome of course seemed the more powerful, for with Herod as its tool, the empire would block any economic reform or political transformation. The poor, of course, were hardest hit by the policies of the empire. The shepherds in *the Christmas story* of Luke are a cipher for the marginalized and the disinherited who have nothing and hope nothing and end in despair. Their fated ending, however, is disrupted by a daring, unexpected new beginning. The poets dare to imagine that in this vulnerable baby, named "save," the power of despair and nullification will be utterly broken. There will be a shattering of the terrifying, deathly power of Herod. The story in Matthew tells of Herod's frantic response (Matt. 2:13), but the hidden event dares to assert that Herod has no chance in this cosmic contest. Into this sordid scene of despairing failure comes

23

the clear voice of the angels, who adjudicate the ambiguous evidence like the referees, who sing of the verdict and the victory of the new baby (Luke 2:10-14).

A fifth retelling (in one of many variant forms) is daily and ordinary. Jesus comes to *the blind beggar Bartimaeus* (Mark 10:46-52). There is nothing cosmic or global in the narrative, except for those who know how to hear the story. In fact the whole of cosmic risk is embodied in this one confrontation for this poor blind man who has reached his last hope. In this moment is poised all the power of despair and darkness and destruction, countered now by this carrier of life. The man says only, "Have mercy." His comrades try to shush him. He says, "Let me receive my sight." Jesus answers, "Go your way, for your faith has made you well." The man sees. His world is transformed. The power of blindness is overcome. The world is under new governance. Of course we thought such a healing impossible. We always think healing is impossible when we have given our trust to Pharaoh, to Herod, to blindness, and to death. In this narrative, however, those old commitments and those tired categories are shattered; there is a new governance!

A sixth retelling, so decisive for the gospel, is *the miracle of Easter.* There is no doubt that the Church's Easter proclamation is invested with cosmic, mythic claims, not unlike the cosmic, mythic claims made at creation and in the Exodus. The miracle of Easter concerns no simply empty tomb or resuscitation. It is rather that God has done battle with the power of death. In 1 Corinthians 15, Paul appeals to the oldest, common church affirmation to assert,

> The last enemy to be destroyed is death. For "God
> has put all things in subjection under his feet."
> (1 Cor. 15:26-27a)

That earliest confession, now taken up by Paul, asserts that all of creation is now freed for life as God's good, joyous creation. The victory wrought over death is hidden, for none of us and none of these ancient witnesses has seen what happened on that hidden Saturday. We only know that in that secret struggle, everything has been changed. New life is indeed possible.

A seventh retelling, classical for Paul, is *the conflict between the work of the law and the power of death, and the gift of vindication by*

24

God's grace. This retelling is so familiar to us that we fail to notice that the metaphor of the courtroom is agonistic, i.e., justice is an adversarial procedure, much as the contest with Pharaoh or the Babylonians was adversarial. According to Paul, in this Jesus, the courtroom is transformed. The guilty are judged by new criteria and the old verdicts are thrown out. There is an acquittal, a pardon, a release from the power of guilt, law, and death, which echoes the liberation from Pharaoh, Nebuchadnezzar, and Herod.

Notice that in all these tellings, many tellings, and retellings, there is no single normative telling. All the tellings, in different ways, concern a deep dispute and a surprising outcome. Notice that none of us nor any of our contemporaries was present in the moment of dispute and outcome. The dispute and outcome happened in places where we have not been and in time when we were not present. These are the many retellings of the story of God's life in the world. They are tellings that assume polytheism, i.e., competing, conflicting powers.

Moreover, in these many retellings, the surprising outcome of victory has always to be won and re-won and won again, each time not just as an echo or replication, but as a newly scheduled contest. Each time that struggle could go either way. In this first scene, the Bible has enormous realism. It acknowledges the resilient power of evil which relentlessly seeks God's defeat.[4] There has not yet been complete defeat of the resilient power of evil. There have been only battles along the way, from which we take heart. The first scene in evangelism consists in the many, many stagings of this hidden struggle in which the governance of our future and the future of the world is at risk. In each retelling, we are assured once again of a clean verdict that overrides the ambiguity of the data. That clear verdict, however, is unfinished, so that there will need to be many more retellings, reenactments, many more disputes and outcomes, for the conflict is quite unfinished and not decisively resolved. Each time we retell, and each time the victory is won, we imagine it is the ultimate telling or the ultimate victory. In our experience, however, there is always required another telling, another verdict, another miracle. Without "another," we die.

THE ANNOUNCEMENT OF VICTORY

In the second scene of the drama of evangelism, there are *the voices of the announcers*, the messengers, the evangelists, who have as their work the daring, artistic rendering of these struggles and outcomes. The task of the announcers is to make the dispute and outcome available, credible, and effective for those who were not present at the event. The announcers are those who, by their rhetorical courage, can show how the outcome there matters here, how the verdict then matters now. Notice that the news is *mediated* by the messenger; it is characteristically not "immediate." It is not directly experienced as a present tense happening, but is relayed. We rely completely on the testimony of the announcers to reconstruct the reality for us which we have not directly experienced.

In *the liturgy among the gods*, the announcer is unidentified. It is the voice of the text, but the text seems to instruct heavenly messengers, i.e., angels. They are clearly voices from the locus of the cosmic conflict who come to the distant, earthly arena of human public life. Thus the text instructs;

Say among the nations, "YHWH is King!" (Ps. 96:10)

This announcement, authorized by the new government, is like the announcement of a successful political coup. It is a report on what has already transpired among the gods as a result of which Yahweh is to be feared, honored, and obeyed among all the gods. That event has happened and it has been decisive. Only when the speaker speaks, however, do the nations know the outcome. They have received the "evangel" from another time and place. The messenger announces that the world is now under new governance. The announcement is not unlike the sweaty announcement of Secretary Haig which was widely perceived as a usurpation of power: "I'm in charge here!" The gospel is announcement that God has seized power in yet another territory.

In *the Exodus event*, the combat between Yahweh and the gods of the empire has permitted the slaves to go free. The message of that outcome is carried by Miriam and the other women who take their tambourines and dance the new reality:

"Sing to YHWH, for he has triumphed gloriously;
  horse and rider he has thrown into the sea."
  (Exod. 15:21*b*)

All who see and hear the dance are now given access to the changed public reality about which Miriam sings. The good news announced is that horse and rider, symbols of military power, have been thrown into the sea; the power of the empire is broken. Life can be reorganized into new modes of power and social relationships. It is the singing women who announce the outcome to those who were not direct witnesses to God's defeat of Pharaoh.

In the construal of *the crisis in exilic Isaiah*, we are never quite told where or when Yahweh had defeated the Babylonians. The defeat has happened in the law-suit scenario of the poet (e.g., Isa. 41:21-29); it has also happened in the public arrival of Cyrus and the Persians (cf. 41:25, 43:14, 44:28, 45:1). However the defeat has happened, the messenger, the one unidentified, comes with the verdict and the message. That messenger has run all the way from Babylon to Jerusalem with the news:

How beautiful upon the mountains
  are the feet of the messenger who announces
    peace,
who brings good news,
  who announces salvation,
  who says to Zion, "Your God reigns." (Isa. 52:7)

He runs and gasps and is barely able to say, "Your God reigns" (52:7). His message is a quotation from Psalm 96:10. The messenger announces the outcome of the struggle. In so doing, he makes effective what has happened elsewhere, which transforms social reality here. God's victory has the capacity to make a decisive change here, however, only when the outcome is uttered effectively and is heard. In that moment of speech, Jerusalem can be free because the power of Babylon is broken. Jerusalem does not know and cannot act on the new reality, however, until the messenger arrives.

Note well, the victory of God by itself does not constitute the drama of the evangel. The telling and retelling is a distinct act, not

27

to be confused with the victory itself. It is the telling as a distinct act which effects, enacts, and makes available the victory. It mattered not at all that Babylon was defeated until the Israelites heard about the defeat.

In *the Christian narrative of Luke 2*, we are given no access to the victory of Yahweh which lies behind the announcement of the angels. We have only been told of the visitation of angel Gabriel to Elizabeth and Mary concerning the birth and its cosmic implication. The innocence of the narrative is framed in an ominous way. On the one hand, the entire birth process happened "in the days of Herod." On the other hand, the name of the angel is Gabriel, i.e., "God's mighty warrior." Thus the issue in the narrative does not concern a virgin birth; the issue is joined between the power of Herod and the counter-power of Gabriel, between the gods of death and Yahweh's power for new life.

The message is announced by the messenger-angel:

> But the angel said to them, "Be not afraid; for see
> — I am bringing you good news of great joy for all
> the people: to you is born this day in the city of
> David a Savior, who is the Messiah, the Lord. This
> will be a sign for you: you will find a child wrapped
> in bands of cloth and lying in a manger."
> (Luke 2:10-12)

Then all of Gabriel's colleagues in the heavenly choir (army) join in singing the victory and outcome into an announcement:

> "Glory to God in the highest heaven,
>   and on earth peace among those whom he
>   favors!" (v. 14)

The good news travels fast. The transformative event happened elsewhere, beyond the narrative. We are not told how King Jesus came to power. That outcome in any case is carried by the messengers and announcers into the fields where the shepherds have been quite unaware that their reality has been decisively changed, completely without their involvement, consent, or cooperation. They only receive the news of the decisive change that has been wrought which affects them.

In *the narrative of Bartimaeus*, as with many of Jesus' transformative interventions, the transaction from event to message is much more immediate. Even in this narrative, however, we can see the same structure to the drama. Bartimaeus has asked for sight. Jesus' own mouth is the carrier of the message of the good news. Jesus says,

"Your faith has made you well." (Mark 10:52)

I do not want to press the model I propose, but one may ask what these words intend. If we think theologically, then I suggest Jesus announces that God, unbeknownst to Bartimaeus and to us, has entered into combat with the power of blindness. Jesus does not do anything. He is the announcer, the evangelist. He only announces the new reality which has happened elsewhere.

In *the Easter narrative*, the news is abrupt and massive. "He was raised on the third day" (1 Cor. 15:4). This is the church's oldest rendering of the news. In the Corinthian credo, we do not know whose voice this is which testifies. It is the oldest, primal voice in the church, the voice of the women at the tomb, of Peter, of the disciple whom Jesus loved, of the two on the road to Emmaus, all of the above. Paul names the witnesses who give the news (vv. 5-7), and finally names himself as on "unfit to be called an apostle" (v. 9). These witnesses speak with one voice. Christ has been raised from the dead (v. 20). The witnesses were not present at the victory, but we rely on their account. In their speaking, the world is decisively changed. So Paul concludes as our most recent witness, "Thanks be to God who gives us the victory through our Lord Jesus Christ" (v. 57).

Paul's theology is a reflection on *the victory of God over the power of death*. That victory has happened in Jesus. Paul must use many metaphors to speak the reality that has occurred in Jesus. What interests us now, however, is that Paul is an apostle (Rom. 1:1, 5; Gal. 1:1).[5] He is the one sent, He is the one sent to the Gentiles. He is the one sent to proclaim, announce, and mediate the theological verdict already established, the transformation already enacted elsewhere. Paul's message points to transformative events

29

beyond Paul's own horizon. Nonetheless, Paul is able to assert in one of his lyrical flights:

> For I am convinced that neither death, nor life, nor angels, nor rulers, nor things present, nor things to come, nor powers, nor height, nor depth, nor anything else in all creation, will be able to separate us from the love of God in Christ Jesus our Lord. (Rom. 8:38-39)

That is all the church received from Paul. The church received Paul's message; the transformation to which he witnesses has happened elsewhere in the gospel, but it matters decisively in the here and now of Corinth and Rome and Galatia.

THE LIVED APPROPRIATION

The first scene is the *decisive combat* to which we have no immediate access. The second scene is *the announcement which mediates* the victorious and outcome, so that it is effective in new times and places. The third scene is the reception of and response to the news, i.e., *the lived appropriation* of the new reality now announced. This third scene is much more open-ended in the several accounts, because the reception, response to, and appropriation cannot be commandeered, programmed, or predicted.

The message is variously received by those who have spent long times letting the news of the changed reality reach, permeate, and saturate various aspects of their lives. The lived appropriation is not easy or obvious, because it requires ceding governance of our life over to the new victor now announced. The ceding over is scary, because we do not know what the new governance entails. And besides, it is far from clear that the authority of the old governance has been fully broken. Our response thus is a mixture of many things, including fear, tentativeness, and powerful wistfulness, sometimes enacted as reluctance.

The response of the nations to the gospel of Psalm 96:10 ("YHWH is King!"), a message voiced from *the victory among the gods*, is one of exuberant doxology and gratitude. How could you respond to the gospel, were you a tree or a mountain or a sea? This is how they received the news of the gospel:

> Let the heavens be glad, and let the earth rejoice;
>> let the sea roar, and all that fills it;
>> let the field exult, and everything in it.
> Then shall all the trees of the forest sing for joy
>> before YHWH, for he is coming,
>> for he is coming to judge the earth.
> (Ps. 96:11-13*a*)

The sea roared its approvals of the gospel message, because the sea had nearly died under the pollution of the gods of death. Now the sea, believing the news, knows that pollution will end. The trees applauded the new governance, because they had heard the chain saws of death and knew that all would be cut down. Now the trees are safe and can get on with their proper fruitfulness. The fields dance; they had nearly suffocated from the chemical fertilizer. Now they can be taken with their own seriousness. The good news is that with the victory of Yahweh, all creation is now freed (as it had been groaning in travail like slaves in Egypt); all creation is now authorized, to be its best true self, functioning as intended by the creator who is creation's best guard and guarantor. The news assures that the power of the gods of death has been decisively broken.

The lived appropriation of *the Exodus gospel* is among the most developed themes of the Bible. Miriam and the liberated women have finished singing. Israel made its troubled way to Mt. Sinai where it faced the new world generated by the gospel of Yahweh's victory over the empire of the Pharaoh. Israel was stunningly aware that the old modes of social relations in the empire would not do in this new, gospelled world.[6] At Sinai, Israel received the commandments, the requirements and permits for new life in the gospel. The ten commandments, the working documents for covenanted community, touch every phase of Israel's life, concerning worship, leisure time, sexuality, economics, political and juridical relations. No aspects of Israel's public life was exempted from Yahwistic redefinition at Mt. Sinai. Appropriation of the gospel

31

concerns the recharacterization of human life and the restructuring of human power and resources in public and personal spheres, according to the governance of the new sovereign.

The task of appropriation of the news is an unending one. Thus Israel's torah is open-ended, under continuing renegotiation and reinterpretation.[7] Moses always has one more interpretive comment to make to Israel. Long after Israel left Sinai, it arrived at the Jordan, ready to receive the land of promise. This was the moment for which Israel had waited and for which Israel had left the empire. At the Jordan, Israel paused for thirty-four chapters of Deuteronomy, while Moses one more time revisioned the promised land as a land of covenantal possibility. He reminded Israel over and over that the strong and the weak are bound and bonded to each other in a common burden and a common destiny. Unless that common bonding is honored and enacted, the land will be forfeited, and Israel will end up back in bondage. The victory of Yahweh and the defeat of the empire makes covenantal social relations of production, distribution, and consumption not only possible, but also urgent and imperative.

Appropriation of the gospel in *exilic Israel* required long, hard work. The messenger, the one with the beautiful feet, asserted, "Your God reigns" (Isa. 52:7). The first reception of the news is singing in joy (Isa. 52:8-9). Then there is the authorization to exilic Israel, "Depart, depart, go out from there" (Isa. 52:11). The exiled Israelites are free to leave the definitional world of Babylon and go home to their proper place, their proper social definition and practice. The gospel permits people to go home from alienation and displacement. Going home, however, is tricky and demanding. Israel cannot go home to the old home, nor can any of us. For that old home no longer exists as we knew it. The gospel requires and permits going home to a new home. Isaiah 56-66 offers a vision of Israel's homecoming, in light of God's staggering emancipation. Israel's appropriation of the news in Isaiah 40-55 entailed the hard work of community-building asserted in Isaiah 56-66, refashioning the fabric of social relations. The work of community-building turned out to be much more difficult and demanding than might be expected from the initial lyrical singing.

The text of Isaiah concerning the return of the exiles starts out with the central decision of appropriation. This is the first thing Israel has to say about the reception of the news of the gospel:

> Thus says YHWH:
> Maintain justice, and do what is right,
>> for soon my salvation will come,
>> and my deliverance be revealed. (Isa. 56:1)

I will mention only two decisions that were faced and resolved in the lived appropriation of the gospel, decisions which concerned exactly justice and righteousness.

First, in Isaiah 56, returned Israel decided that it must of necessity be an inclusive community, welcoming all foreigners and eunuchs, and that its worship would be for "all peoples" (v. 7). There was a strong urging that such people were disqualified, because they were not "like us," because they had sexual disqualifications, because they had been allied with the oppressive empire. In this text at least, a large vision of social alternative prevailed, and all who wanted to share in that large vision were invited into the community.

Second, in Isaiah 58, there is conflict over religious scruples. The urging of the text is that the religion and piety required in light of the gospel are essentially a practice of neighbor love that concerns the attentiveness of the strong to the needs and well-being of the weak. Notice how the voicing of religion inevitably spills over into political-economic questions of responsibility and entitlement:

> Is not this the fast that I choose:
>> to loose the bonds of injustice,
>> to undo the thongs of the yoke,
>> to let the oppressed go free,
>> and to break every yoke?
> Is it not to share your bread with the hungry,
>> and bring the homeless poor into your house;
> when you see the naked, to cover them,
>> and not to hide yourself from your own kin?
>> (Isa. 58:6-7)

These assertions in Isaiah 56 and 58 envision a gospelled community that is in drastic contrast to the Babylonian world which had no such commitment to justice and righteousness. Indeed, the empire can never have such commitment, because it is ordered and legitimated by gods who have no such interest. Israel is mandated otherwise because its God, subject of the news, has from the outset been a God who cares primarily about neighbor relations. The gospel is the news that distorted patterns of power have been broken; the reception of the gospel is the embrace of radically transformed patterns of social relationships.

In *the Christmas story of the gospel narratives*, the appropriation of the gospel news from the angels by the shepherds is laconic. They "returned, glorifying and praising God for all they had heard and seen" (Luke 2:20). Luke does not give us much, and I will not overstate. The act of giving glory to God, however, is no small matter. Indeed the catechism recognizes praise to be our "chief end." In its understated way, the narrative suggests that the shepherds in this Christmas moment had arrived at their chief end in life. The shepherds were moved and permitted a new, energized worship. They now acknowledged a new sovereignty in their lives, which in every case requires the abandonment of other sovereignties. Moreover, the subversive act of praise, which Luke characteristically values, is because of what they had "seen and heard." What they had seen and heard was nothing less than the emergence of a new reality in the midst of their need and deprivation. The shepherds are among the first witnesses, who, when they see Jesus, grasp in an inchoate way that the old world had been invaded, occupied, and transformed.

Beyond the initial response, of course, Luke's birth narrative and the response to the birth is not limited to the shepherds. The story of the birth is positioned in the Gospel story to initiate the much larger account of healing power unleashed in the Lucan narrative. The gospel announced by the angels and received by the shepherds reverberates among many people who have their lives dislocated and regrouped by this king sung to power by the angels. All through the gospel story, multitudes, tax collectors, and soldiers are driven by the gospel to the question, "What shall we do?" (Luke 3:10, 12, 14). It is the question of appropriation of the news.

The response is practical and concrete, though for each constituency different: share a coat with him who has none, collect no more than is properly yours, rob no one by violence or false accusation. The news of the angels anticipates utterly transformed social relations.

The appropriation of the news in the Gospel of Luke of course spills over into the story of the church in Acts. That narrative account concerns a community kept in crisis by the new governance, always seeking to find adequate and obedient response. The account in Acts, like the ongoing interpretation of Deuteronomy, shows the community regularly filled with power, and regularly in tension with the authorities.[8] All of that power and tension is already adumbrated in the initial Christmas narrative.

In *the narrative of the healing of Bartimaeus*, the fresh appropriation of the news is, as is characteristic with Jesus' magisterial interventions, brief and to the point. The appropriation is in two parts. First, "immediately he regained his sight" (Mark 10:46-52). He saw! It was a gift and his situation was deeply and immediately transformed. It was a gift, but wrought through his faith, through his trust, through his courageous insistence. The second statement in the narrative flows directly from the first: He "followed him on the way" (v. 52). Bartimaeus becomes a disciple. Since Mark has Jesus and his disciples "on the way to Jerusalem," this terse note suggests that Bartimaeus now, in his changed circumstance and his new resolve, accompanies Jesus on his costly way to death and resurrection.

The Easter announcement, rooted in the church's earliest testimony and interpreted by Paul, culminates in an ethical appeal. The proclamation of Easter news is not an end in itself. Its end is the generation of new life in the world:

> Therefore . . . be steadfast, immovable, always excelling in the work of the Lord, because you know that in the Lord your labor is not in vain.
> (1 Cor. 15:58)

The community convened in Easter has much work to do. Indeed, most of Paul's letters to Corinth concerns exactly the work that this gospelled community is to do. In 1 Corinthians, as it now stands, the summons at the end of chapter 15 is immediately followed in 16:1 by reference to the contribution for the needy, a theme handled Christologically in 2 Corinthians 8. Resurrection faith with its cosmic claims, leads to an active practice of generosity and compassion, surely the Lord's own work that is to be done by the community that receives the news.

The Pauline announcement of news in Romans and Galatians is cast as vindication through graciousness. This announcement leads, in Paul's argument, to new ethical possibility. As is well known, the connection between the sounding of the gospel and a new life of obedience is dramatically structured into the epistle to the Romans. Paul asserts in 8:28-29 that we will not be separated from God's love because that connection is sustained from God's side. Promptly, it follows:

> I appeal to you therefore, brothers and sisters, by the mercies of God, to present your bodies as a living sacrifice, holy and acceptable to God, which is your spiritual worship. Do not be conformed to this world, but be transformed by the renewing of your minds, so that you may discern what is the will of God — what is good and acceptable and perfect. (Rom. 12:1-2)

The church is empowered for transformed life in the world, authorized to act counter to the ways of the world. In sum, the community which hears the news is invited to a life of hospitality (v. 13) as a way to counter a world bent on vengeance (v. 19).

The same move from news to ethical appropriation is given in the letter to the Galatians. The news is liberating:

> For freedom Christ has set us free. Stand firm, therefore, and do not submit again to a yoke of slavery. (Gal. 5:1)

The liberty of the gospel is an invitation to walk in the spirit and to produce the fruit of the spirit:

> The fruit of the Spirit is love, joy, peace, patience,

kindness, generosity, faithfulness, gentleness, and self-control. There is no law against such things. And those who belong to Christ Jesus have crucified the flesh with its passions and desires. (Gal. 5:22-24)

Again it is clear that the ethical appropriation of the gospel is against the un-gospelled life of the world which lives in bondage, by the flesh.

A RECURRING, PATTERNED DRAMA

My argument thus far is an attempt to trace something of a taxonomy of evangelism. I am aware that my argument is excessively schematic and at some points forced a bit for the sake of the taxonomy. I do not believe, however, that this proposed schematization overstates or skews the data of the text itself. I have developed my argument this way because I want to insist on two primary points. First, evangelism is *a three-scene drama* in which each scene must be kept distinct from the others. Our common propensity is to collapse everything about evangelism into the second scene of announcement.

The data I have assembled indicate two important features concerning this dramatic sequence. On the one hand, the announcement and the announcer do not participate in and are not present to the first scene, the actual conflict and victory. The conflict and victory happen elsewhere, beyond our access. On the other hand, the lived appropriation does not follow from the announcement easily, readily, or automatically; rather the appropriation is difficult, costly, demanding work.

Second, the entire drama of evangelism is *definitionally unfinished* and must be rendered repeatedly in all its parts. The gospel is not a "done deal" when its dramatic character is understood. It is a deal always to be done again in the face of resilient evil, distortion, and alienation. Each rendering of this drama is as urgent, dangerous, and costly as any other enactment of the gospel. The Bible is the continual reenactment of this dangerous news. The church is the community that continues to participate in this drama and to insist that the drama is the definitional account of its life in the world. It is important that the drama not be reduced to a single telling, because such a reduction is false, both to the biblical witness and to the experience of our own life. The taxonomy I propose, then, is presented on the facing page.

Now my purpose is not simply to review the data of the biblical account. My intent is to explore what that taxonomy will look like in our own situation of faith and ministry. Obviously, when one seeks to extend and contemporize the taxonomy, one must take some risks. I do not imagine that my model will be immediately acceptable to all, and we will make different judgments. I intend at least that my proposal may provide for all of us an angle of vision and a contribution to our critical conversation. Thus I will propose a contemporary implementation of the taxonomy in all three scenes which are discrete and unfinished.

I will begin with *scene two*, which is perhaps the most obvious, the announcement. The announcement in our context of faith and ministry must, in my judgment, be concrete, uncompromising, and Christological. Thus, the lean announcement is that in Jesus Christ, God has overcome the power, threat, and attraction of the power of death. That is our theme. I suggest that this clean, clear, lean statement is scarcely negotiable. There follows from that simple statement several notations.

First, this linguistic act of proclamation is epistemologically subversive.[9] The assertion makes no accommodation to the reason of this age; I submit that this language of the gospel is affrontive to liberal and conservative alike, because the claims are too radical for liberals and too comprehensive for conservatives.

Second, the language of the gospel is essentially dramatic. It permits and requires that historical reality be presented as agonistic. This in itself is an important gain for theological discernment. Note well, however, that this language is not congenial to any of our reductionisms. This language invites no creedal scholasticism and does not especially serve "the Reformed Tradition." It anticipates no moralism that permits either complacency or self-congratulations. It allows no psychologism that offers inner peace or tranquility. The agonistic language of the gospel is brusque, harsh,

38

A Taxonomy of Evangelism

	I. The Hidden Victory	II. The Announcement	III. The Lived Appropriation
Cosmic Encounter	Yahweh vs. the Gods (Ps. 96:46)	"Horse and rider he has thrown into the sea" (Exod. 15:21)	"Let the heavens be glad" (Ps. 96:11)
The Exodus	Yahweh vs. Pharaoh (Exod. 1–15)	"Your God reigns" (Isa. 52:7)	The Covenant at Sinai (Exod. 19–24)
The Homecoming	Yahweh vs. Babylon (Isa. 46–47)	"Horse and rider he has thrown into the sea" (Exod. 15:21)	"Maintain justice and do what is right" (Isa. 56:1)
Christmas	Yahweh vs. the empire (Luke 2, Matt. 2:13-18)	"To you is born this day ...a Saviour" (Luke 2:11)	"Glorifying and praising God" (Luke 2:20)
Jesus' Ministry	Yahweh vs. blindness (Mark 10:46-52)	"Your faith has made you well" (Mark 10:52)	"He followed him on the way" (Mark 10:52)
Easter	Yahweh vs. death (1 Cor. 15:54-55)	"Thanks be to God, who gives us the victory" (1 Cor. 15:57)	"Be steadfast, immovable, always excelling in the work of the Lord" (1 Cor. 15:58)
Paul	Yahweh vs. Satan, sin, and death (Rom. 5–8)	"Neither death nor life... will be able to separate" (Rom. 8:38-39)	"Be ye transformed" (Rom. 12:2)
Our Situation	Yahweh vs. the deathly power	God in Christ has over-come the power of death	Freedom for an alternative life of neighbor love

and not "user-friendly." It follows, I suggest, that such a claim requires in most of our churches, liberal and conservative, a changed universe of discourse to permit the dramatic power of the claim to be either spoken or heard.

Third, there is no doubt that succinct, verbal articulation is crucial. This dramatic assertion permits two important extrapolations which might still be regarded as announcement. On the one hand, the announcement invites daring artistic inventiveness in music, art, and dance to portray the agonistic character of our faith. On the other hand, the claim may be proclaimed bodily, by action and risky intervention where the power of death pervades our common life. Thus an act which embodies the news may be reckoned as announcement.

When we move back from the second scene of the announcement to *the first scene* of conflict and victory, we are required to ask about the conflict in which God has emerged victorious. We must ask, where does the power of death show its terrible, powerful face in our context? Now things get sticky in making an answer. I submit that for people in our culture and in our churches, death operates in the seductive power of consumer economics with its engines of greed; in the mesmerizing of military power and its production of fear, insecurity, anxiety, brutality, and a craving for vengeance; in the reduction of all of life, human and non-human, to a bartering of commodities, until we and our neighbors are all perceived as means and not as ends.[10] That is, the central conflict with the gospel in our time has to do with socio-economic, political practices which bespeak theological idolatry, an idolatry which has come to exercise sovereignty over most of our life.[11]

The seductive, dominating power of these values is not an economic mistake, a political accident, or a military miscalculation. It is rather the work of the power of death which is having its relentless way among us. In tilting the gospel toward socio-economic, political matters, let it not be imagined that I am introducing a category that is "liberal" or partisan or new or modern. Indeed, all through the Bible the gospel has been exactly and precisely concerned with social relations related to power, goods, and access. Indeed, there is almost no aspect of the biblical presentation of the gospel that is otherwise. The issue, however, is not finally socio-economic or political. It is theological. It concerns the power for life and the power for death and the struggle between them for our life, our loyalty, and our imagination.

The victory of God in our time over this deathly idolatry is hidden from us, as God's decisive victory is always hidden from us. We do not know exactly when and where that victory has been wrought. It is hidden in the weakness of neighbor love, in the foolishness of mercy, in the vulnerability of compassion, in the staggering alternatives of forgiveness and generosity which permit new life to emerge in situations of despair and brutality.[12] It is hidden in the cross where it is always hidden, and in all subsequent manifestations of the power of the cross. The news grounded in God's victory is that the deathly power of commodity has no claim upon us, no legitimacy to define our life. We are free of its awesome power and claim, and are therefore free to live a different life.

The shape of the conflict and the victory is crucial for what is announced. The announcement in scene two must be rendered in full concern for social criticism, with attentiveness to socio-economic, political reality. The announcement is not innocuous palaver about easy, obvious, agreed upon matters; the announcement is always an act of liberated defiance which challenges and exposes the defeated power which still appears to have vitality and authority. Thus the announcement of victory is marked by risk. It asks listeners to believe what is not self-evident, and to trust and act against what still appears to be our self-interest. The announcement asserts a victory which is not self-evident, but which invites people to take a risk on the basis of a less than obvious verdict.

This hidden victory and this daring announcement touch all aspects of our life. I have no doubt that the killing power of commodity worship touches every phase of our existence. It touches public economic questions of third world debts, but it also touches sexual intimacy and the crisis of family life. It touches the large anxiety of public, international security and it touches local anxieties about intergenerational conflict. It touches large despair about the intractable problem of homelessness which is so massive that we can hardly address it, and it touches small despairs of broken communication with loved ones. It touches every dimension and every fabric of creation. In the midst of our massive seduction and sell-out stands the gospel and its messengers.

Finally, consider *the third scene*, the act of lived appropriation. The reception of the gospel has an emotional dimension, that we should be "moved" to new life. The impact of the gospel, however, is not mere emotionalism. It is a decision, reached abruptly or dawned upon slowly, that we can and may and must disengage from the power of death. There may be a quick conversion, but there is no easy conversion, because conversion means to be uprooted from a fabric of meaning and security to which we are long habituated. Anyone who imagines easy embrace of the news, I imagine, is romantic about the cost of newness, or uninformed about the danger and risk.

The crisis of lived appropriation called slaves to leave the safety of Egypt and they soon yearned to return (Num. 14:4). The crisis of lived appropriation called exiles in Babylon to depart, while the empire seemed still to have all the rewards we most crave. The birth announcement of Bethlehem may have caused the shepherds to jeopardize what little solace they found in the mutton market in Rome-authored Jerusalem. The gift of sight requires Bartemaeus to assume fresh responsibility for his life and to make new decisions for himself. Many of us, beset by the "tortured conscience of the West,"[13] find the power of inordinate duty and distorting obligation so massive that it endlessly skews our life.

Lived appropriation of the news in our context, I suggest, consists in finding ways to disengage our life, our bodies, and our imagination from the seemingly all-powerful world of consumer pursuits, of self-serving arms, of self-satisfying brutality, because the God known in Jesus offers an alternative to the ordering of life around commodity greed. All of us are deciding how far to go, how fast to go, how daring to go, how radical to go with the news. Some will appropriate the news in radical ways through civil disobedience. Some will more modestly face simpler forms of living. Some will reorder finances, sexuality, and child nurture in alternative ways. Not everyone will do the same, and some will resist completely.[14] There is no law or prescription or even sure guideline about specifics. Indeed, the lived appropriation of the news is never law, but always invitation, never coercion, but always authorization and permission.

It is the evangelical task of the church to invite people into this daring drama, to keep this odd, revolutionary conversation available and credible in our life. It is evident to all of us and to each of us that this is a counter-conversation about "a more excellent way." On many days we are passionately committed to "a less excellent way," a more mediocre way that we do not want to have countered. The news of this alternative way is not scolding or reprimand or demand. It is invitation. It is permission. It is celebration. Entrusted to us is the conduct of this unfinished counter-drama, in which all may participate.

THREE PRACTICAL IMPLICATIONS

There occur to me three practical issues that derive from my analysis, upon which I will make brief comments. First, the hackneyed business about a dichotomy between *"evangelism" and "social action"* is fundamentally misguided. It will not do to divide the issue in this way. It is a false issue without foundation in the Bible, fashioned by people who refuse to think about evangelism theologically. On the one hand, if we take only "evangelism" as this dichotomy has it, we are left with the question, "News for what?" The answer is, news for alternative obedience in the world. That is what the news of the evangel is all about, and any evangelism that does not go toward this radical lived appropriation is fraudulent.

On the other hand, if we take "social action" as it is featured in this dichotomy, we are left with the question, "Social action from what source and for what end?" The answer is that social action comes from the radical news of God's new governance over the world, and social action is witness and praise to the new governor. Any social action which is not rooted in the news and aimed at the new ruler has no claim upon biblical warrants.

Our work is to overcome this dichotomy. To do that, we need both. Both what? Both *the news* and *the appropriation*. We cannot have announcement without appropriation or appropriation with-

43

out announcement. If the gospel concerns changed governance, then that changed governance concerns all of life, for the victory of God over death is not a victory in some selected zones of life, but over all of creation and against every threat of chaos. Thus our appropriation of the news concerns civil rights and sexuality, birth and death, national defense and family nurture. The church now has the hard work of finding language to override the seductive dichotomy which permits ideology to fence off zones of life from evangelical impact. I imagine we shall find that liberating language only by a return to the root text and its dramatic idiom.

Second, the subject of evangelism invites false disputes between *liberals and conservatives*, which is not quite the same as "evangelism versus social action." It will not do for the church to use such ideological labelling language, for such labels betray our notion of the wholeness of life under the singleness of God's purpose. With so-called conservatives, I agree that we must get our language right, to affirm that our evangelical language is for us realistic language, and we must not blink at the epistemological embarrassment of the gospel. With so-called liberals I agree that we must see that our unembarrassed, realistic evangelical-Christological language is not isolated, specialized language, but is public language concerned with public issues, uttered for the sake of public criticism and public possibility. Whenever liberals shrink from *the epistemological scandal* of the gospel and whenever conservatives shrink from the *public dimension* of the faithful language of the evangel, the gospel is distorted and the Bible is misread.

I submit that in our time, so-called conservatism is an attempt to reduce the danger of the Bible to confessional safety, and so-called liberalism is an attempt to avoid the dramatic system-shattering claim of the gospel. I submit that so-called conservatives and so-called liberals might well return to the shared, concrete language practice of the Bible to learn again that the utterance of the name of God (or the name of Jesus) is endlessly subversive, polemical, risk-taking. Indeed, I suggest that our scholastic debates about liberalism and conservatism are simply smoke screens to protect our vested interests and to fend off the danger and threat of the gospel. Or conversely the reduction of the gospel to our favorite political slogan is a refusal to let the unfettered news of

God have its say. The gospel news of changed governance in all of creation is more radical, demanding, and empowering than any of us can readily imagine, embrace, or domesticate.

Third, evangelism is related *to church growth*, related but in no way synonymous. In speaking of evangelism, one must speak of church growth, but only at the end of the dramatic process, and not any sooner. Evangelism is never aimed at institutional enhancement or aggrandizement. It is aimed simply and solely at summoning people to new, liberated obedience to the true governor of all created reality.[15] The church is a modest gathering locus for those serious about the new governance. There must be such a gathering, and such a meeting, and such a community, because the new governance is inherently against autonomy, isolation, and individualism. The church grows because more and more persons change allegiance, switch worlds,[16] accept the new governance and agree to the unending and difficult task of appropriating the news in practical ways. "Church growth" misserves evangelism, however, when the church is allied with consumerism, for then the church talks people out of the very obedience to which the news summons us.

There is no easy way about the relation between evangelism and church growth in our society; established as our church is, I am not romantic about the enormous difficulty. I suspect that the two central ingredients required of us now are these: first, we must recover *gospel modes of discourse* which are not moralistic, dogmatic, scholastic, or pietistic, but relentlessly dramatic. Second, we must recover *the focal drama of baptism*, which is a subversive act of renunciation and embrace. The claims of the gospel of God's hidden, decisive victory are fully voiced in our language and in our baptism. We are, however, mostly so kept and domesticated that we cringe from the very news given us. We find ways to skew our language and trivialize the sacrament so that there is nothing left for us except accommodation to cultural expectation.

I care greatly about the well-being of the institutional church, its health, its budget, and its numbers. I fear the growth of secularism which marginalizes the church; I fear equally the greedy religious right-wing which is only a chaplain for commodity militarism. I genuinely care and fear as I visit churches and see them frequented largely by older people; it is like visiting Wilder's *Our Town* in a season of despair a generation later.

In our moments of sanity, however, we know that the issues of evangelism do not concern the health of the institutional church. The issue is rather that the life of creation, the fabric of the human community, is deeply in jeopardy among us. The crisis concerning evangelism is a "world question" and not a "church question." Our common jeopardy is very large in terms of arms and chemicals, terror, and massive international indebtedness. The jeopardy is very local in terms of drugs and violence, fear, greed, and isolation. That old world of alienation can not much longer be propped up, either by the military will of the super-powers, or by the economic coercion of the markets, nor by well-meaning ideology that passes for religion. We are in enormous jeopardy, a jeopardy that is common to us all, and there are no mirrors any longer with which to deceive ourselves.

Now imagine that to us — the band of slaves, the company of exiles, the stunned disciples in Jerusalem, the lean apostles in the Roman empire — to us here has been given a clue, an invitation, a possibility of new life:

> Then turning to the disciples, Jesus said to them privately, "Blessed are the eyes that see what you see! For I tell you that many prophets and kings desired to see what you see, but did not see it, and to hear what you hear, but did not hear it." (Luke 10:23-24)

To us, an alternative: hidden, weak, foolish! The gospel asserts this high Christological claim against all pretense of the world. To this little flock is given a clue about a more excellent way. That extraordinary clue is immediately followed in Luke's gospel by the parable of the Good Samaritan. That story ends, as you know, with the magisterial closure:

> The one who showed him mercy. . . . Go and do likewise! (Luke 10:37)

The large claim of the authority of Christ (vv. 21-24) is linked to the concrete practice of neighbor love (vv. 25-37). Word here becomes flesh, sovereignty becomes compassion, weakness becomes strength, foolishness becomes wisdom, suffering becomes hope, vulnerability becomes energy, death becomes life.

Imagine the church as the place for an alternative conversation. In a society of denial, as the church we speak what we know, evoke resistance and yearning, permit alternative, authorized newness. As liberals and conservatives, we could settle for shared acknowledgment that the church is this relentless conversation, bearing witness to the news in the face of all brands of fear and ideology.

The subject of the evangelical conversation is how our life, our bodies, and our imagination can be weaned from the deathliness of the world to the newness of life in the gospel. It is a conversation to which all are invited. From our several enslavements we are summoned to a common, liberated obedience. That conversation is difficult and unfinished. It is a conversation that promises our life shall come together in wonder, love, and praise. What news!

Outsiders Become Insiders

In the three chapters that follow, we shall be concerned with the ways in which dramatic "news events" in scripture concern various "constituencies" which are candidates for membership in Israel's covenant. Through a variety of texts, different constituencies are invited to share in the drama which we have articulated in chapter 1. In this chapter we consider, first, the most obvious constituency for evangelism, the *outsider* who stands apart from this "community of news," who lives by other narrative identities, and who has no "membership" in Israel's narrative world.

While other texts also concern the "outsider," I have chosen to consider Israel's relation to the outsider in the book of Joshua and in particular, in the great meeting of Joshua 24. This relationship to the outsider in the meeting of Joshua 24 is a quite complete and tensive one. There are, to be sure, conflictual arrangements in the book of Joshua whereby Israel is commanded to "destroy the Canaanites." Israel's efforts in this regard issue in what we roughly refer to as "the conquest." Obviously in such a perspective, evangelism aimed at outsiders will not get very far.

While the historical issues behind the book of Joshua are complex and obscure, scholars have noticed that in "the central hill country" around the city of Shechem, there was no "conquest," no armed confrontation with the inhabitants of the land, but seemingly a relatively peaceful coexistence between these communities.

It will be useful for us to reflect more precisely upon the meaning of the term "Canaanite," the word used to describe non-Israelites in the land. It is clear that in these texts, "Canaanite" is not an ethnic term and does not refer to a tribal or ethnic group. Indeed the "Israelites" themselves likely were "Canaanites" with a peculiar religious identity. In the materials of Deuteronomy and Joshua, the term "Canaanite" is a polemical, ideological term. It refers to those in the land who are committed to exploitative, non-covenantal social relations (i.e., economic and political), and who practiced forms of religion (so-called "Canaanite religion") which may have given symbolic legitimation to non-covenantal practices. (Since Israelite texts are ideological and polemical, I am here describing a paradigmatic use of the term "Canaanite" as used in the texts, and not offering an historical description of the "Canaanites.") That is, "Canaanites" are those who are committed to social practices which are viewed as hostile to the covenantal vision of Israel. There is a strong current of scholarly opinion which suggests that the "Canaanites" are "urban elites" who control the economy, and who enjoy a powerful political advantage, to the detriment of the food-producing "peasants" who understand themselves as "Israelites." Suffice it to say that such social practices and religious commitments would hardly be amenable to Israelite faith claims.

Now this way of understanding "Canaanite" offers us a model for evangelism of "outsiders." In that ancient time and in our time, outsiders (= Canaanites) may be those who are committed to (or trapped by) socio-economic practices at variance with covenantal ethics, who practice religious symbolization that supports such practices. Without suggesting any easy equivalence, such "Canaanite practices" may have a counterpart in social relations of exploitative greed, systematically arranged through tax and credit laws, which are legitimated by the ideology (theology) of the free market system. I do not intend here to be polemical, but only to make a sharp contrast between exploitative systems of values and covenantal faith, and to suggest a parallelism with what the texts mean by "Canaanite."

Posed in this way, our question of evangelizing the "outsider" comes down to this: How can such a person who lives in a different (antithetical) way legitimated by a different ideology be made a full participant in the story and the life of Israel?

The text from which we will seek an answer to our question is Joshua 24. In this text, we are invited into a meeting where Joshua authorizes folk to make a decision, either to live life in covenantal ways legitimated by the God of the covenant, or to live another kind of life legitimated by "other gods" who are very different from Yahweh. It is this choice that permits outsiders to become insiders. As insiders shaped by a different story, the neighbor is differently perceived, and a different God becomes the decisive shaper of reality. I consider that three outsiders entertain Israel's three classic memories and thereby embrace a new life:

- a young woman from a dysfunctional family;
- a tired business executive; and
- a member of the permanent underclass.

These are all candidates to become transformed insiders!

♦   ♦   ♦

Not much is known about the meeting at Shechem in Joshua 24. The meeting is set at Shechem. This very ancient city was in part of the land where there had been no "conquest," i.e., no intense social conflict. The Israelites apparently had lived peaceably among other inhabitants. The other inhabitants there had been unchallenged and uninterrupted by the intrusiveness of the Israelites and by the claims of Yahweh. The picture is of a peaceable coexistence between Yahwistic zealots and the old, settled population that had not yet thought about Yahweh.

The dominant voice in this meeting is that of Joshua. I suggest four aspects of the character of Joshua which may interest us. First, his name means "save," as in "You shall call his name Joshua, for he shall save his people." Joshua offers a rescue and a deliverance to this assemblage. Second, Joshua was no eyewitness to the great saving events to which he testifies. It was Moses who was the eyewitness. Joshua is one generation removed; he is simply a child of the tradition, having heard the story, trusting it enough to repeat it. Joshua is not unlike Paul: "For I handed on to you as of first importance what I in turn had received" (1 Cor. 15:3). This meeting is part of an ongoing traditioning process. Third, he is a person utterly pledged to torah obedience, because he believes that such torah obedience will secure the land and generate a good life. His speech in this meeting is an offer of torah-obedience to the uninterrupted lives of the Shechem community. Fourth, Joshua's authority and credibility is grounded in his earlier act of great courage, when alone with Caleb he was willing to trust Yahweh against seemingly great odds (Num. 14:6-9). It is this act which legitimates him, though he is formally ordained by Moses.[1]

Scholars believe that this chapter is pivotally situated in the final form of the biblical text.[2] It stands as the culmination of the story of the Hexateuch (i.e., Genesis — Joshua), the conclusion of the story of God's rescue mission for Israel. Just before this chapter in Joshua 21:43-45, it is asserted that all of God's promises to Israel have been kept; now Joshua invites the outsiders at Shechem, the ones who have not yet participated in this narrative, to become insiders to the story. Thus this is an act that intends to textualize this community into a new, alternative text, so that the world may be reimagined and re-lived through the memory of Israel.

FROM A TROUBLED, DYSFUNCTIONAL FAMILY

We do not know who was in the assemblage with Joshua that day in Shechem. It is reported that it was "all the tribes of Israel," the leaders, heads, judges, and officers. Elsewhere in a like meeting, the list is more comprehensive, "the people — men, women, and children, as well as aliens residing in your towns" (Deut. 31:12, cf. Neh. 8:1-2). This was a large, inclusive, comprehensive meeting, for Joshua believed that the offer of these alternative memories was urgent for all of the population, was available to all, and could be appropriated by all.

We cannot, however, pay attention at this distance to everyone at the meeting. Instead I will imagine with you three specific listeners at that meeting, listeners addressed by Joshua, listeners who could be contemporary with us, but who likely were not very different, even in those days. Notice how, in my rendition, I move from text to imagined listener. It is the text that creates the listener.

Joshua begins his extended address with an allusion back to *the book of Genesis*:

> Long ago your ancestors — Terah and his sons Abraham and Nahor — lived beyond the Euphrates and served other gods. Then I took your father Abraham from beyond the River and led them through all the land of Canaan and made his off-spring many. I gave him Isaac; and to Isaac I gave Jacob and Esau. I gave Esau the hill country of Seir to possess, but Jacob and his children went down to Egypt. (Josh. 24:2*b*-4)

Joshua takes a very long sweep of the ancestors, because his faith is deeply rooted. It begins with Terah, father of Abraham. He and his sons worshiped other gods. But Abraham journeyed, and then Isaac, and then Jacob and Esau. This is all familiar stuff, and may have been familiar to the people of Shechem who had not heard of the Exodus. There is however, so much in the crevices of the Genesis narrative to which Joshua does not even allude, but which an informed listener would have heard anyway.

In the mention of these ancestors, we may note two recurring themes from that memory. On the one hand, the mother Sarah, along with the mothers Rebekah and Rachel who come after her, were all barren. They could not get pregnant, could not have a child, and so had no assured future. In generation after generation, at the last moment, in the fullness of time, God worked the impossible, gave an heir, created a future when none seemed available. It is a memory to evoke astonishment. On the other hand, in every generation there was intense sibling rivalry, especially over land and water: Ishmael and Isaac, Esau and Jacob, Joseph and his brothers. The quarrels were intense, because the disputes were about security and well-being into the future. (That is what land disputes are always about.) Remarkably, in each generation, the younger, unentitled child made a claim and received the inheritance. This is the tale of the first becoming the last and the last becoming the first, and the folk of Shechem heard this odd story on that day.

In the midst of the tension between the sons and brothers,

however, we may notice a counter-theme in this story to which Joshua alludes. There is in the face of these tensions over land and water a family sense. When Abraham died, Ishmael and Isaac together bury him and share the inheritance (Gen. 25:9). When Isaac died, Esau and Jacob shared in the death (Gen. 35:29). And when Jacob died there is a moving scene of reconciliation among the sons (Gen. 50:15-21). In spite of conflict, this is a family whose members cannot cease to interact and to care for each other.

Both major motifs, the impossible births and the impossible reconciliations, evidence a special family. Genesis tells of a deeply troubled family. Through the narrative, however, the trouble is matched by a healing purpose that addresses the family, gives hope, offers futures, and heals along the way. What dominates Joshua's brief telling of Genesis is the triple use of the word "gave":

> I gave him Isaac. . . .
> I gave Jacob and Esau. . . .
> I gave Esau the hill country.

There is a giver; this is a story about a gift. There is a power and a presence at work to give newness, to break the vicious cycles of barrenness, fear, alienation, and hostility.

To be sure, we do not know who was listening to Joshua that day in Shechem. Let me nevertheless commit an act of anachronism. One of the listeners that day who came from the uncontested territory of Shechem, one of those who came to hear the memory for the first time, was a young woman. She lived in a troubled, dysfunctional family. In that family were endless wars and disputes over turf, unsettled accounts over old confiscations. Her family could not get past the wars. She rightly perceived her family situation as helpless, hopeless, and impossible. She saw that it was not only hopeless for her, but that it was an impossible destiny for her siblings and for the generations yet to come, unto the third and fourth generations. She lived in despair.

Imagine the interface that day in Shechem — between a helplessly troubled family and a story of another family, equally hopeless but visited, intruded upon, made new, given an unmerited future. It is an alternative story told and retold, very old and now on the lips of Joshua, now told and heard at Shechem. As the young woman listened, she entertained the story as a counter-tale of her own life and that of her family. In her hearing, it dawned on her that her family was not without the giver, not without the gift, not without an overt act of newness. What she heard that day from Joshua was a tale of a possibility whereby God breaks hopelessness, reconciles siblings, guarantees futures, gives safe land. God does what this family or any family cannot do for itself. As she listened, she found the weight of despair being lifted as she decided against that very despair.

A TIRED BUSINESS EXECUTIVE

In his proclamation, Joshua moved quickly. He handles the Genesis memory in only three verses (vv. 2-4). Then Joshua is abruptly into *the Exodus narrative*:

> Then I sent Moses and Aaron, and I plagued Egypt with what I did in its midst; and afterwards I brought you out. When I brought your ancestors out of Egypt, you came to the sea; and the Egyptians pursued your ancestors with chariots and horsemen to the Red Sea. When they cried out to YHWH, he put darkness between you and the Egyptians, and made the sea come upon them and cover them; and your eyes saw what I did to Egypt. Afterwards you lived in the wilderness a long time. (vv. 5-7)

The rendering of the Exodus event also does not take many verses, but what a story! The account is dominated by the first-person statements of Yahweh who emerges as the key player in the drama. This Yahweh visited Israel through the human agents, Moses and Aaron. This same character in the drama, Yahweh, takes on the empire, the savage monopoly of power and authority. In the chaotic waters this invisible holy one, this utterly free and unpredictable one, takes on the empire with its arms of horses and chariots. By any rational reckoning, the empire would prevail against the slave community.

Yahweh, however, is like a wild card in the deck. It turns out that the empire cannot always prevail, because there is a freakish freedom in the historical process that has not yet been domesticated. This holy power brought Israel to the edge of the chaotic waters and there Israel watched its future in astonishment.

Israel, this little community of the powerless, was at great risk. It had learned to conform silently to the empire and to its requirements and objectives. And now, Israel broke the silence. In fear and daring, Israel cried out. It announced itself and its hurt. It broke the silence and made a large demand on the holy power of heaven. The wonder of the narrative is that the cry from below evoked the power of God from above. In response to the slave cry, God moved the darkness and the sea, God mobilized creation on behalf of the needy slaves, God managed the chaos redemptively. They were freed, as they never expected to be!

The narrator cannot quite make up his mind about the story. Did the exodus happen to our ancestors, for he says "I brought your ancestors out of Egypt"? Or did it happen to us who now listen, for in the same verse the narrator says, "You came to the sea." The sentence is, "I brought your ancestors out of Egypt, you came to the sea." It is always "them" and it is always "us," always then and now, always there and here, concerning all of this community of telling and listening through time.

There are odd things indeed in this core memory that Joshua retells. It is a class reading of historical reality, a match between the dominant empire and the docile slaves. The story tells of a mighty, inexplicable miracle whereby the dominant empire has its authority broken. Yahweh emerges as a real and powerful character in this Israelite rendering of reality. There are three players in the drama, not two: empire, peasants, and God. The other oddity of this narrative is that the holy power of God is triggered by the cry of the peasants who break their docility and find their voice, and require Yahweh to come to be present in the crisis of bondage.

We do not know who was listening that day in Shechem. But let me commit a second anachronism. One of the people in the assemblage that day was *a tired business executive* who worked in the brickyard. He was not an Egyptian. He was one of the peasants. Because he was conscientious and productive, he had been made a foreman, trusted by the Egyptians, given power and authority as a middle-management guy. He was trusted by the Egyptians and commensurately despised by his own people. The overriding reality of his life was the brick quota, day after day. He lived a good life, because he ran a good brickyard.

In his daily round, however, he had noticed two realities. First, payment of his mortgage depended on his continued enmeshment in the imperial system. He could not let up for a minute, or he would lose everything. He also noticed that each time he met the quota of bricks, they upped the numbers and drove him even harder. That is, he had to keep at production with ever increasing intensity. He was trapped and there was no way out. He was exhausted and no longer cared about his work, but he kept going through the motions. He thought often that he despised how his life had been caught. He counted how he had twelve years and thirteen days until retirement. Twelve years is a damn long time, and even thirteen days is too much to bear. He had become a eunuch of the corporation, and he knew that to get along he had to produce and conform, every day of his life.

Joshua's retelling of the Exodus narrative refuses to accept any of this despairing resignation. The narrative starts reality at another place. It views the empire not as the great provider, but as a deathly nemesis. It tells about a new character in the drama, this Yahweh, who had not been known by the workers, and not reckoned with by the empire. Nonetheless, the first utterance in this narrative is "I," a new I which generates a fresh community of pain and hope. Upon hearing this tale, our company robot notices; this story defies docility, urges pain to be spoken, dares to break into the tea party of the empire, and gives authority where there has been none. This wearied man noticed that the story is not a pious religious account, but it is about economic power and jobs and security and exploitation. He noticed that the story is very dangerous, and the summons from docility is uncompromisingly abrupt.

As he listened, however, he received a fresh glimpse of his hopeless conformity. Joshua had uttered the phrase, "I brought you out." The man had already known himself trapped with no way out, and now hears the word, "I brought you out." I brought you out through human courage, through crisis and risk, through holy mystery. As a result there is now life untrapped. The man began to ponder that he had been too docile, and it was killing him, and he would try otherwise. He would make the effort because now, in the drama of his life, there is this other One who sponsors a departure. A departure from docility into self-assertion is the most dangerous move he could imagine. He also noticed that the story was honest. It ended with these words: "Afterwards you lived a long time in the wilderness," in the wilderness without all the fringe benefits, in the wilderness without guarantees. He thought it worth the risk; he began to let into his life little gestures of departure that could amount to a massive liberation.

A MEMBER OF THE PERMANENT UNDERCLASS

Joshua does not leave this litany finally in the wilderness. He moves quickly to the third story, the narrative of *the gift of the land*:

> Then I brought you to the land of the Amorites, who lived on the other side of the Jordan; they fought with you, and I handed them over to you, and you took possession of their land, and I destroyed them before you. Then King Balak son of Zippor of Moab, set out to fight against Israel. He sent and invited Balaam son of Peor to curse you, but I would not listen to Balaam; therefore he blessed you; so I rescued you out of his hand. When you went over the Jordan and came to Jericho, the citizens of Jericho fought against you, and also the Amorites, the Perizzites, the Canaanites, the Hittites, the Girgashites, the Hivites, and the Jebusites; and I handed them over to you. I sent the hornet ahead of you, which drove out before you the two kings of the Amorites; it was not by your sword or by your bow. I gave you a land on which you had not labored, and towns that you had not built, and

> you lived in them; you eat the fruit of vineyards and
> oliveyards that you did not plant. (vv. 8-13)

This is the story that Joshua himself knows something about. He had to finish the Moses story, because Moses never saw the promises of Genesis kept, never entered the other side of the wilderness. Joshua had gotten where Moses did not. He knew and told about Yahweh's powerful resolve to complete the story by bringing these daring peasants to their own land. The land to which they came was not empty. It was already claimed; those preexisting claims to the land had to be overcome. There is at the center of Joshua's narrative a tale of land dispute, conflict, aggression, and violence. Later on there would be difficult questions about seizing the land of another. But that is for later on. In the moment of the crisis, the "have-nots" do not worry much about niceties in the midst of social conflict. They have to take what they can, and know that the God of Abraham and Sarah did not want them to be landless for another day. Thus the land of Canaan, Palestine, Israel (note the names) became an arena for violent disruption, as it continues to be. This story is not simply about human conflict. The narrative dares to claim that the Holy God is allied with landless peasants who had to struggle all the day.

The power to bless and curse is crucial. In war, propaganda is pivotal, and the capacity to condemn and denounce the enemy is powerful. For that reason, this cunning king of Moab hires a propaganda officer, Balaam. He employs him to demonize (curse) invading Israel. He cannot curse, however, because when he speaks, his words come out as blessing. It is as though God has jammed the airways. God forces Balaam to condemn the Moabite war effort and to support the intruders. At the center of this story is the God who violates conventions and who gives these nobodies a fresh chance, who gives them a safe place already anticipated in the Genesis narratives.

This narrative section in Joshua's speech ends with an amazing verdict from God:

> I gave you a land on which you had not labored,
> and towns that you had not built, and you live in

them; you eat the fruit of vineyards and oliveyards
that you did not plant. (v. 13)

You have not labored, you did not build, you did not plant. God
grants you what others have built and planted. God lets you have
their stuff; you are, by the doing of God, entitled to it.

We do not know the assemblage of Shechem that day. But let
me commit yet a third anachronism. Among those present was *a
member of the permanent underclass.* He was at the edge of the crowd.
He was unshaven and unkempt, and he dared not lift his head. He
could hardly remember how he had dropped out of the working
middle class, but it was an irretrievable drop. He had listened to
market ideology long enough to believe its claim. He believed that
if you worked, you would prosper. So now his lack of prosperity
was unmistakably his fault. He did not blame the system, but
himself. He was embarrassed, ashamed at this poverty and his
consequent failure in appearance, but he had no power to reverse
the process. He understood his deprived, disadvantaged social
position. While he seethed with resentment, he knew how to keep
in his place. It was a deep, massive wilderness, without any adequate life-support system. He mostly was numbed and came to the
meeting just to be in a crowd, to break the isolation for a moment.
He was, however, scarcely able to listen to the proceedings.

Then, however, he heard Joshua talking insurrection:

> . . . land on which you had not labored, towns that
> you had not built . . . vineyards and oliveyards that
> you did not plant.

No, it was not an insurrection. It was a gift, a promise, an offer.
He knew the deathly ditch of disadvantage, and the offer of
redistribution of goods. It was not a romantic vision, for this is a
story of real social goods. The story smacks of violence, for it
concerns seizing what others had. It is an act of hope, an utterance
about the reversal of disadvantage. It dawned on this bedraggled
man that in this story, unlike the Canaanite stories he so believed,
he was entitled, meant by God, to have and to hold life for himself.

As is always the case with this story, we do not know if the
hearing of this tale of entitlement would lead to violence. Violence

might come, for this story has a potential for violence; it reminds the marginalized of what is their God-given entitlement. Or hearing the story might only generate hope, break the idelogy of deprivation, stir the yearning for entitlement, and begin to authorize liberated self-assertion.

LIVES REDESCRIBED

There was a hush at the end of v. 13 that day in Shechem as Joshua finished the recital of the memory. There was electricity released into the assemblage, as there always is when the stories are rightly rendered. Joshua offers the listeners at Shechem a world of three stories, that is all. In this three-storied universe—

- There is present *a young woman* in a hopeless family situation. She cannot please her family or save it, and she is in deep despair. And what she hears from Joshua is *a new possibility*. Her family, like the one in the story, could be healed and transformed.
- There is in the crowd *a middle-aged business executive*. He cannot satisfy the empire, but he is a convinced practitioner of docility. He is so well off because he conforms in productive ways. What he hears in the speech of Joshua is *a departure*. He ponders breaking his docility enough to move, even at the risk of his current well-being.
- There is at the edge of the meeting *a homeless man*. He is sunk deeply into disorder and deprivation which he reckons to be depravity. What he hears is *entitlement*, a land of enough in which he may hold first-class citizenship.

No doubt there were many others at Shechem that day who heard and perceived their lives differently. But stay with these three who are typical of people who gather to hear the story. They are outsiders who have believed stories of death too long. They have been held in thrall to

- a story of a family set permanently into *dysfunction*;
- a story of an empire with *insatiable demand*;
- a story of *marginality*, with no hope of any alternative.

And now Joshua gathers this dangerous memory:

- the story of *dysfunction is retold as possibility*;
- the story of *demand is retold as departure*;
- the story of *marginality is retold as entitlement*.

These three heard a new story. What they heard that day they had never heard before, or even dared imagine. It was a story which had the holy one as the key actor, and that changed everything else about the story:

- in Genesis, it is the God who causes the *impossibility*;
- in Exodus, it is the God who authorizes *departures*;
- in Joshua, it is the God who *gives towns and vineyards*.

The story offers a new, decisive character. Notice that the new character is scarcely credible and can only be given as a character inside the story. I wonder how these three had come to accept a story of their lives which did not include this character. Ostensibly other stories were accepted because the character of God in the story is not credible in the modern world; such a character is an intellectual impossibility and therefore an embarrassment. More likely, however, the problem is not an intellectual one. More likely the story of this God has been rejected because people of power who defended the status quo had effectively advocated a different story, one without holy purpose and holy power at its center. In that story without holy power and holy purpose,

- the family of the woman was reduced to a story that proclaimed that the dominant truth is our shared dysfunction;
- the executive had been sucked into the claim that Pharaoh is ultimate and Pharaoh knows best;
- the homeless guy had accepted full responsibility for his hopeless lot in life.

Those stories, perfectly credible and without God, robbed each teller and each hearer of any hope or possibility for life.

And now Joshua had reconstructed each of their lives. The startled listeners were not worried about intellectual embarrassment as they heard the new story of their lives. They were drawn and persuaded by the narrative power to imagine themselves differently. They discovered that in hearing this story about God who had never been narrated to them before, they were at the same time given a new story of self. They became, in this moment of new hearing:

- a woman open to possibility;
- a man capable of departure;
- a man now entitled.

That is how it works in these memories, as Joshua understood well. The story of this God is an authorization for a different social practice in the world. The territory around Shechem would never again be the same after Joshua had his say, because all three stories had been told and heard and would reverberate in wondrous and dangerous ways. Because of these stories, all of life is reconstrued. Joshua, teller of the evangel, has as his work the complete and radical redescription of all of reality.

STORY-BASED IMPERATIVES

Now, after the recital, Joshua came to the hard part in his speech (vv. 14-15). The transition in the text is marked by "So what?" "Now therefore," you must do something. The memory impinges upon the present, and Joshua turns the narrative indicative into an urgent imperative.

The imperative is in three parts. First there is a positive imperative concerning Yahweh:

- *fear Yahweh*, i.e., take Yahweh with ultimate seriousness;
- serve Yahweh, i.e., enter into a covenant which acknowledges this single, uncompromising sovereignty;
- fear and serve in "sincerity and faithfulness."

The Hebrew term rendered by NRSV as "sincerity" is *tamim*, which means wholeness, integrity, without division, ambiguity, or reservation. Do it totally and with utter reliability.

The imperatives state as strongly as possible that this choice and this new loyalty must be uncompromising and unaccommodating. But what would such a choice entail? In this urging Joshua intends that the listeners in Shechem should choose the story just recited, and choose the God who operates in these stories:

- Choose the story of Genesis: let the young woman choose a tale of new possibility.
- Choose the story of Exodus: let the business executive choose a tale of departure.
- Choose the story of Joshua: let the homeless man choose a tale of entitlement.

One cannot know Yahweh apart from Yahweh's story, and that story concerns socio-economic, political reality that is transformed by the power of Yahweh's intrusion into the narrative. Choose a new God and choose a redefinition of the world.

Second, Joshua's imperative states a negative which is the price of this positive choice. *Put away* the gods of your ancestors beyond the River and in Egypt. Remove, get rid of other gods. There can be no other loyalties if the story of Yahweh is embraced. This demand is a deep either/or that touches every aspect of life, personal and social, intimate and public.

In Genesis 35:1-4, there is a closely related narrative which speaks of "putting away." Jacob commands his company in a speech at Shechem:

> Put away the foreign god[s] that are among you,
> and purify yourselves, and change your clothes;
> then come, let us go up to Bethel, that I may make
> an altar there to the God who answered me in the
> day of my distress and has been with me wherever
> I have gone. (vv. 2b-3)

Albrecht Alt has suggested that this was a regularly enacted ritual in which there was a pilgrimage from Shechem to Bethel, which dramatically symbolized a change of gods.[3] Interestingly, Jacob hid the foreign gods under the oak that was near Shechem

(v. 4). Shechem, where Joshua holds the meeting, functions in the older tradition as the place where Israel relinquishes the other gods, which are here symbolized by certain kinds of clothing and jewelry. Yahweh cannot be embraced until there is a costly abandonment of other loyalties, other fears, other hopes, and other payoffs.

In the New Testament, I suggest that the boldest parallel to these negative and positive commands occurs in Ephesians and Colossians.[4] In Ephesians 4, the writer issues a sturdy imperative:

> You were taught to put away your former way of life, your old self, corrupt and deluded by its lusts, and to be renewed in the spirit of your minds, and to clothe yourselves with the new self, created according to the likeness of God in true righteousness and holiness. (Eph. 4:22-24)

What is to be gotten rid of is a former way of life, *an old self*, an old identity. What is to be put on is *a new self* according to the holiness and righteousness of God. In the following paragraph, the "putting off" includes falsehood (v. 25), bitterness, wrath, anger, wrangling, slander, and malice (v. 31). In their place are to come tenderheartedness and forgiveness (v. 32). Notice the metaphor of clothing, so that the process of putting off and putting on is like changing clothes. The metaphor is very close to the ritual action of Genesis 35.

The same movement is evident in Colossians 3:5-14. The negative is to "put to death" whatever is earthly: fornication, impurity, passion, evil desire, and greed (which is idolatry), until you "have stripped off the old self with its practices" (v. 9). The positive imperative follows promptly in v. 10: You will "have clothed yourselves with the new self, which is being renewed in knowledge according to the image of its creator" (v. 10). That new self is clothed with compassion, kindness, humility, meekness, and patience (v. 12). The grand conclusion is this: "Above all, clothe yourself with love, which binds everything together in perfect harmony" (v. 14).

These statements about a change of clothes and a change of self are commonly thought to be actions related to baptism. There may have been a dramatic change of clothes to signify visibly a new self. Baptism is a dramatic act of reidentity. Notice that this ritual act is in continuity with the two actions at Shechem, first by Jacob and then by Joshua. The embrace of the God of the Bible and of the gospel entails dramatic, radical, total transformation.

If in Joshua 24 the serving of Yahweh is to embrace the story of Yahweh, then what does it mean to put away the gods of the ancestors? I suggest this requirement means that one no longer lets the stories of the other gods shape identity, perception, or imagination:

- as the young woman embraces this story of possibility, she is to put off the *story of despair*;
- as the tired executive puts on the story of departure, he is to put off the *story of docility*; and
- as the homeless man puts on the story of entitlement, he is to put off the *story of deprivation and disadvantage*.

The changing of gods is the changing of stories, which is the "switching of worlds."[5]

The third imperative of Joshua interests us less. Joshua concludes that if choosing Yahweh seems evil in your eyes, you have two other options. You can choose the gods of Mesopotamia, or the gods of Egypt. Both choices are available. If, however, you choose one of these, you cannot have the narrative of Yahweh just recited. Two things strike me about Joshua's final statement of choice. First, Joshua does not beg or coerce or even try to persuade. He only states the options and requires a decision, but he can live with different choices. Nothing is at risk for Joshua in this reception of the story. Second, Joshua is not impressed by a positive choice or deterred by a negative choice. He himself has no doubt, no critical reflection. He is clear on his own household:

As for me and my household, we will serve YHWH.
(v. 15)

He is free and unencumbered. He is fully committed to the story to which he invites others.

This chapter has begun with Joshua engaged in a powerful reconstrual of reality, according to the classic, evangelical memory of Israel. The good news is that those who hear this reconstrual can rechoose. Nobody at Shechem is stuck with their old loyalties, or the old gods, or their old stories. The young woman therefore is not stuck in despair but can rechoose. The tired executive is not stuck in hopeless docility and conformity, but can rechoose. The homeless man is not stuck in disadvantage and deprivation, but can rechoose. For any and for all, life can begin again at a very different place. The story provides ground for rechoosing, and now Joshua himself rechooses in an unambiguous life-giving way.

A NEW, COVENANTAL IDENTITY

We can discuss the remainder of this Shechem encounter more briefly. After reconstrual and urgent invitation, comes the hard, sober act of reckoning. Joshua warns Israel and the other listeners to weigh their decision carefully. The listening community responds to Joshua immediately with a vow and a commitment, and a determined resolve. They will not forsake Yahweh (v. 16). The other gods will hold no attraction. Indeed, this gathering has listened well, because in vv. 17-18 they say back to Joshua the narrative of vv. 12-13, by making references to the Amorites. These eager listeners accept the new story. They understand that Yahweh belongs crucially in this narrative of deliverance and fulfillment; now they confess that they also belong in this story. Finally, after the recital in vv. 17-18, the verdict is asserted at the end of v. 18:

> Therefore we also will serve YHWH, for he is our
> God.

By implication, "We are Yahweh's people," belonging to none other.

This decision, however, is hard and serious and dangerous. Joshua will not permit any easy, facile choice. He presses them to consider well that this choice of Yahweh is a dangerous, freighted act, because this obedience is not easy. Joshua reminds the new adherents that Yahweh is impossible to serve, because Yahweh is holy, jealous, and unforgiving (v. 19). This is no easy religion, no cheap grace, no comfortable welcome. If you sign on, the expectations are tough, the demands are relentless, and the threat of judgment is ominous.

In response to the heavy warning of Joshua, the community is adamant:

> We . . . will serve YHWH. (v. 18)
> No, we will serve YHWH! (v. 21)
> Yes, we are witnesses against ourselves. (v. 22)
> YHWH our God we will serve, and him we will
>   obey. (v. 24)

This is a rapid-fire exchange between Joshua and the assembly. Joshua keeps trying to talk the assembly out of joining this story; the congregation, conversely, keeps insisting that it understands the risks and wants into the story nonetheless.

It is worth noting that this is a peculiar conversation to have in the midst of our theme of evangelism, especially with one eye on growth. This is a dramatic and ominous moment when *outsiders become insiders*, but they do so at the risk of their lives. In fact, against our common notion of inviting and persuading people who may be reluctant to come in, this text presents outsiders eager to come in, and Joshua the doorkeeper seeking to prevent and discourage any facile decisions to enter the story of Yahweh and Israel.

It is on this basis of the insistent pledge of the community that Joshua takes the decisive act of covenant-making:

> So Joshua made a covenant with the people that
> day, and made statutes and ordinances for them at
> Shechem. (v. 25)

The entire passage has been building toward this decisive moment.

Four items may be noted in this action of Joshua. First, this community is bound irreversibly and inextricably to the character of and purpose of Yahweh. Yahweh is now bound inextricably and irreversibly to this people. Yahweh will never again be people-less, and this community can never again be Yahweh-less. While that bonding is an assurance, it is a costly assurance. It requires commitment on the part of the community to the things for which Yahweh cares most deeply, which as we have already observed, includes hope for the barren and dysfunctional, freedom for the burdened, and entitled land for the marginated. In this oath of allegiance, the new insiders pledge to care intensely about these matters known only through these identity-giving narratives.

Second, the way of this binding relation is covenant. That means a trustful kind of mutuality. Covenant is not a contract between two autonomous partners who can stand in power alone, but it is a relation which frees each in vulnerability to receive life from the other, to be postured in mutual dependence. Such a step affirms that in entering covenant, Yahweh becomes a God like none other, and Israel becomes a people like none other (cf. Deut. 4:7-8).

Third, this mutual commitment entails a rejection, not only of the other gods and their stories, but also the rejection of their gifts, i.e., gifts of self-sufficiency, control, and self-aggrandizement. It is no wonder that Joshua resists any easy covenant, because the requirement of this covenant include the denial of much else that the world takes to be valuable and legitimate.

Fourth, Joshua finally gets down to cases, as he provides statutes and ordinances for Israel. That is, in a role imitative of Moses, Joshua places Israel under a stringent and specific obedience. He issues commandments. When one joins Yahweh, one accepts the weighty obedience. The laws of Yahweh's covenant are not heavy-handed legalism; they are not petty self-serving moralisms. They are rather boundaries and limits which define the horizon of covenantal humanity. The laws are to guard each one's dignity and save each one's pride.

It is neither necessary nor possible here to pursue the obligations that belong to this enactment of the Gospel. As you know, the obligation consists of love of God and love of neighbor. I suggest that in the first three commandments of the decalogue, "love of God" means that God is an end and not a means. God has no utilitarian value. That holy power encompassing the world cannot be harnessed into our interests and idealogy. Conversely, commandments five through ten are an assertion that the neighbor is an end and not a means, that the neighbor is not to be utilized or manipulated or harnessed into our interest, ideology, or program, but is to be respected, honored, and esteemed for his or her own sake. And as Patrick Miller has shown, the fourth commandment on the sabbath brings together love of God and love of neighbor, because both God and neighbor are entitled to rest.[6] It is the sabbath that refuses a utilitarian approach to either God or neighbor, that entertains a different vision of both heaven and earth.

In this moment of oath-taking, the community at Shechem takes for itself a peculiar identity and vocation in the world, and in the land of Canaan. In the ancient world and in the contemporary world, this decision is for a risky existence, for this is a community that refuses the cunning exploitative ways of the world. In this act of covenant making, all of life is brought under Yahweh's particular sovereignty; nothing is held back. This sweep of sovereignty includes *family*, as in the case of the woman who heard the alternative model of family in Genesis. This sweep of sovereignty includes *economics*, as in the case of the executive who found a model of liberated economics in Exodus. This sweep of sovereignty includes a *redistribution* of land, as in the case of the homeless man who heard the offer of Joshua. The core zones of existence — family, economics, land — are brought under the sway of new governance. The zones of freedom, security, responsibility, and sufficiency are all now differently characterized.

This formation of a new community is marked in our narrative by the enactment of a public moment. In that moment, the new community asserts for all to see that this is now a community of very different intentionality. All three outsiders have signed on as insiders. They embrace the world of the three stories of possibility, departure, and entitlement. In this three-storied universe, God is heard and trusted differently. The neighbor is differently affirmed, and the world is taken as a place where covenantal mutuality prevails. The alternative to this covenantal mode of existence is the gods beyond the river who give only despair, docility, and disadvantage. Joshua-folks endlessly "put off and put on," are clothed in covenant, clothed in baptism, clothed in new obedience, clothed in their rightful minds. To "deal falsely" (v. 27), against which Joshua warns, is to slide from covenant into the deathly world of the outsider. The role of the insider is demanding but healing and finally life-giving. That is good news indeed. For to love brother and sister in covenantal ways is to be raised to new life — new life for members of dysfunctional families, new life for exhausted agents of the empire, new life for hopeless marginals, new life in a new season of hard listening and ready answering (cf. 1 John 3:14).

Joshua 24 is rooted in some historical happening at Shechem. It occupies a crucial place in scripture, however, not because it is an important historical report, but because it is a paradigm for such a transformative meeting that may happen again and again. The "map" of "Canaanites" and other outsiders becomes "Israel-ites," i.e., people allied with Yahweh and committed to the neighbor practice of covenant, is a "map" that is germane to contemporary issues of evangelism. Commitments to "Canaanite" (i.e., non-covenantal) social relations legitimated by the gods of greed and indifference are not remote from us. Thus this meeting conducted by Joshua is given for many re-happenings and repli-cations, which are the canonical intent of the text. In these re-happenings and replications, folk are invited into these alter-native memories, alternative promises, and alternative com-mands. It is never an easy meeting. The invitation, nonetheless, permits an embrace of a very different life, the "cost and joy" of which are known only by insiders.

Forgetters Made Rememberers

We now take up a second constituency for evangelism, namely *insiders* to the faith who have grown careless, weary, jaded, and cynical about the faith. It is obvious to anyone that "outsiders" to the faith should be a proper aim of evangelism. It is not so obvious that insiders also need evangelizing. In this chapter, we consider the ways in which insiders are a prime constituency for reincorporation into the vitality of faith.

In the world of ancient Israel, the community of faith had been given by God the wondrous gifts of the land — security, abundance, prosperity, and well-being. Two texts, the sermon of Deuteronomy 8 and the poem of Jeremiah 3, reflect upon that wondrous gift of well-being and its potential seduction.

The ancient voices of Moses and Jeremiah understood that everything for Israel depends upon the power and availability of its core memory, a memory that kept Israel close to, reliant upon, and responsive to Yahweh, the God of liberation, covenant, and land. Those same voices, however, understood that well-being in the land is a likely enemy of that core memory. In a context of affluent prosperity, Israel would eventually forget its memory, scuttle the God of the memory, disregard the demands of that God, and forfeit the joy of covenant with Yahweh. Moreover, this forgetting jeopardizes the very existence of Israel. As a consequence, insiders to the covenant become hollow and uncaring, honoring empty forms of faith and practice, but completely cut off from the gifts, demands, and joys that belong to this relationship.

The text we consider in detail, Nehemiah 8, comes at the end of this process of forgetting and forfeiting, and seeks to reincorporate these hollow insiders into the power of the faith. The programatic reincorporation enacted by Ezra revolves around three non-negotiable claims. First, even if it has been forgotten, this community has its life from the *torah-scroll*. By this time in its life, Israel is a "people of the book." It must stay close to the book so that its imagination keeps in purview the gifts and demands of God. Second, reincorporation involves a deliberate, intentional, *substantive reengagement with the core memory*. Israel's self-identity is not simply a generalized inclination, but it is specific, ordered around particular miracles which are known and recitable, and which redefine reality. Ezra requires discipline in rereading the text in order to recover that memory, now forgotten both by people and by leaders. Third, the "re-texting" of Israel in the Festival of Booths means that a return to the scroll and to the memory is not a cognitive one in didactic fashion. Rather, Israel must *bodily reexperience and reenact* the memory, recovering its vulnerability in bodily exposure.

In this extraordinary act Ezra intends that insiders should be reincorporated into the vitality and "bite" of the faith which began in news. I suggest that the analogue of the crisis in the time of Ezra for the current U.S. Church is readily apparent. The "crisis for insiders" in our churches is that abundance and affluence have caused church members to be distanced in self-sufficiency from the power and cruciality of the memory so that the church suffers from profound amnesia, even among those of us who vigorously go through the motions. To the extent that the analogy works, this drama of reincorporation suggests for our time and place:

- a *"back to the scroll" movement* which is not scholastic in its intent, but which entertains the wild images and awesome possibilities of the scriptures as life-defining;
- a disciplined, intentional relearning of the specific, detailed substance of the memory, with an awareness that these specificities touch every aspect of our life, both for joy and for obedience; and

- *a bodily act of vulnerability*, so that the claim of this memory touches our "bone marrow" in unmistakable ways.

Indeed, I imagine that the evangelizing of insiders (i.e., most of the whole of the Western church) may be our primary agenda in evangelism. What becomes clear in this text is that "Ezra wasn't kidding!"

THE MEETING WITH EZRA

There is a second meeting given us in Nehemiah 8, not unlike the meeting at Shechem in Joshua 24. This meeting seeks to do the same sort of thing as did that meeting, but there are important differences. Unlike Joshua 24 which stands at the beginning of Old Testament tradition, the meeting in Nehemiah 8 stands at the close of Old Testament narrative. Unlike Joshua 24, this meeting is not, as at Shechem, what is for Israel a newly explored territory. The meeting is in the familiar and beloved context of Jerusalem, at the Watergate. Unlike Joshua 24, which comes at the end of great buoyancy from the triumphant work of Joshua, this meeting is held at the far edge of exile, when Jews came back from exile to the pitiful, shabby ruins of destroyed Jerusalem. The meeting therefore is not in a mood of buoyancy, but in the wake of desolation. Unlike Joshua 24, the key figure in the meeting is not Joshua who stood so closely connected to Moses, but it is now Ezra. Ezra is very far removed from the root events of Israel's memory. Nonetheless, in the completed tradition he is reckoned to be the second founder of Judaism (after Moses), or indeed its genuine founder. Quite like Joshua, Ezra also must bear testimony to memories which go far behind his own remembered experience.

Most important and crucial for the argument I will make is the fact that, unlike Joshua 24, this meeting does not concern persons invited for the first time into Israel's covenantal faith, but it concerns Jews who are already deeply rooted in the tradition. This is not a story of outsiders now being made insiders (as in Joshua 24). This is a story of forgetters being made rememberers. You will rightly conclude that I believe this to be the second urgent task of evangelism. Ezra is preoccupied with the work of inviting the community already pledged to faith, back to a serious embrace and practice of that pledged faith.

The work of the meeting conducted by Ezra is straightforward and simple. Here (unlike Joshua 24) the people take the initiative and gather themselves together. They instruct Ezra to read the scroll. Two characteristics of this meeting are worth noticing. First, the meeting is inclusive, men and women, all who were old enough to understand (vv. 2-3). This assemblage is not so formal and official as in Joshua 24. It sounds more egalitarian, and it intends to involve the entire community. Second, the activity of the meeting is reading the torah in the hearing of the community.

There are two sorts of concerns in this reference to torah. The first concern is technical: scholars debate about what was in this scroll. Some think it was the Priestly stratum of the Pentateuch, i.e., late priestly instruction about right worship. Others believe it was the completed Pentateuch or something very close to it. In either case, the actual formation of the Bible we now have was well along. What was being read is normative core literature which became the Pentateuch.

The second concern is more important: our English rendering of torah as "law" is mischievous and problematic. The word "law" scarcely catches the point of the reading. "Torah" means the entire written and cherished normative memory of the community, all the lore and narrative and poetry and song and old liturgy that had formed and shaped and authorized the imagination of the community. In rabbinic sources, moreover, it is later urged that there is also an "oral" torah alongside what is written. The reference to "law" smacks of a Christian stereotype of Judaism which grossly misrepresents it. The mistaken stereotype entails two severe costs. On the one hand, it does a disservice to Jews and Jewish practice. On the other hand, it cuts Christians off from the vitality and dynamic of the torah enterprise which could make a positive difference to us Christians.[1]

This reading and hearing of the torah was in fact a communal reappropriation of a core memory that had been forfeited, neglected, trivialized, or scuttled. In this act of rehearing, the community of belonging Jews, men and women, was being regathered and reconvened as a community of glad, liberated obedience.

It is most important to note that the torah was not only read and proclaimed; it was interpreted (*meporash*) (v. 8). This means that there was exposition, commentary, translation, appropriation, and application, so that compelling connections are made between old tradition and present circumstance. This old text of Israel's memory never exists as authoritative for the community without imaginative interpretation.[2] This scene in Nehemiah 8 is regarded in the tradition as the moment of the founding of Judaism, as the moment in which Jews became a "people of the book." It should be noted, that this people becomes in this convocation the people of the *interpreted* book, so that the old text continues to impinge upon imagination with vitality, authority, and contemporaneity.

What happens in this dramatic encounter with the text is that the imagination of Judaism, so impacted by the power and ideology of a series of demanding empires, is being rescripted around a peculiar textual tradition often not known, not valued, and not understood. The founding of the community happens through bold rescripting of communal imagination.

I propose now to go behind this meeting which is perhaps dated 458 BCE (though that dating is only one of three critical options). What had happened that made this moment necessary, and what made it possible? I shall consider three texts as guidelines for understanding the theological, liturgical crisis of post-exilic Judaism. I shall not be asking historical questions, though the broad sweep of historical circumstance will be clear enough. Rather I shall be reflecting on the textual emergency that the Bible traces as a theological problem. I intend of course to point to the textual emergency that constitutes our own urgent context of evangelism.

A GIFT AND A WARNING: DEUTERONOMY 8:1-20

This sermon placed in the mouth of Moses is an exquisite piece of torah theology. It reflects upon the connection between torah appropriation and a life of well-being and security. It believes that obedience to torah is the *sine qua non* of public well-being.

Twice Moses makes a solemn appeal for serious adherence to the torah (vv. 1, 5-6). Israel is a community of obedience and its very future depends upon obedience. "Obedience" has gotten a bad press out of authoritarian social practices and especially authoritarian religious traditions. That, however, is not what this tradition is about, and we need to work intentionally against such easy stereotypes of the Old Testament.

The obedience to which Israel is here summoned, as is characteristic for Israel, is situated within and supported by a narrative memory (vv. 3-4). In this brief retelling, Moses invites Israel to remember (v. 2). Israel is to remember the wilderness as a time of testing, a time of risk and need, and a time of God's faithful, generous care. In that time, Israel becomes aware that it could not store up life securities, but it had to depend in the most precarious way upon the daily grant of life from God given as bread from heaven. Moreover, Israel is to remember that for forty years of terrible leanness, there was an odd, inscrutable sustenance: food was given, clothes did not wear out, feet did not swell. God's sustenance had been for them fully sufficient. The triad of food, clothes, and feet is not unlike the triad of life, food, and clothes in Matthew 6:25-32. "God knows what you need, so do not be anxious." Israel's memory concerns the ways in which God's attentive generosity overwhelms Israel's anxious need.

The generosity of God is stated in a lyrical statement of extravagant well-being:

> For YHWH your God is bringing you into a good
> land, a land with flowing streams, with springs and
> underground waters welling up in valleys and hills,
> a land of wheat and barley, of vines and fig trees
> and pomegranates, a land of olive trees and honey,
> a land where you may eat bread without scarcity,
> where you will lack nothing,[3] a land whose stores
> are iron and from whose hills you may mine cop-
> per. You will eat your fill and bless YHWH your

God for the good land that he has given you. (vv.
7-10)

It is all pure gift! God is the subject of the important verbs:
God is bringing, God has given. And between these two verbs, is
a good land — streams, springs, wheat, barley, vines, fig trees,
pomegranates, olives, honey, iron, copper — everything to fill and
to bless. This is a new creation! Because God gives extravagantly,
Israel comes to a land of abundant life. Thus the promise of the
sermon is juxtaposed with the old *memory* of vv. 2-4 and the lyrical
anticipation of vv. 7-10. Both witness to sufficiency, security, and
extravagance of Yahweh as the context for torah obedience.

In v. 11, the sermon turns to imperative and warning (vv.
11-20). The sermon knows that prosperity causes amnesia. The
good, generous blessing of the land will cause massive, programmatic forgetting.

There are warnings about forgettings (vv. 11, 14, 17). The
speech plays two rhetorical elements against each other. On the
one hand, vv. 12-13 look back to the blessing of vv. 7-10: fine
houses, herds and flocks, silver and gold, everything multiplied.
On the other hand, vv. 14-16 look back to the memory of vv. 2-4,
concerning the God of the Exodus who made water from rock and
sent bread in the wilderness. The juxtaposition shows rhetorically
how present affluence drives out the sensitivities of gratitude.
Gratitude has a very tough time in the midst of unlimited affluence.

The reason is that when one can no longer remember a lesser,
more precarious time, all present benefits appear to be not only
absolute, but also self-generated, making gratitude unnecessary,
impossible, even silly. Moses warns that a forgetting people should
not become self-congratulatory and say, "My power and the might
of my own hand have gotten me this wealth" (v. 17). There is then
no one to thank. And if there is no one to thank, then there is no
one to heed, no one to obey. In an instant one becomes autonomous, self-sufficient, self-admiring, self-congratulatory, not ac-
countable to anyone. This sermon of Moses is psychologically
perceptive; it sees clearly how wealth and well-being oppose a
capacity for gratitude.

The sermon ends with a powerful appeal and a dire warning

(vv. 18-20). The appeal and warning are an urgent call to remember. Remember the power of gift that has been offered in vv. 7-10 and 12-13. Remember that you are recipient and not generator. Then the positive appeal turns to ominous warning: "If you forget . . . you will surely perish."

Such a warning is not fashionable among us. The warning in any case needs to be purged of any facile supernaturalism. This is not a threat that if God is not worshiped, God will swoop down from the sky and terminate. Rather Moses understands the moral dimension of the political process. If Israel, birthed in liberation (Exodus) and situated in covenant (Sinai), forgets these memories, it will very soon start playing the old power games of Egypt, and start practicing brick quotas again in order to get ahead by the standards of the empire. And when Israel is seduced back into those games, the option of freedom and the alternative of an egalitarian covenant community will be given up. "To perish" does not mean God will act supernaturally to destroy, but that the daring social experiment in the world which is Israel will disappear, not by divine assault, but by social seduction and erosion. Israel will have been talked out of its peculiar vision of reality and its daring practice of another way in the world, talked out of it without even noticing that it is happening. Israel will disappear as an option to the world, not by force, but by careless default. "To perish" is not to be assaulted, but to give up one's theological identity for a quick fix of well-being. It is to trade the birthright of covenantal social relations for a mess of pottage, a perennial temptation for the community of this radical faith and daring social practice.

Moses lays down the options and dangers that will vex Israel as it enters the land of prosperity. Everything depends on a live memory. Everything is jeopardized by careless forgetting. Everything rides on remembering and forgetting. The indispensable remembering to which Israel is urged is quite explicit, concrete, verbal, and stylized. Israel's future depends on this unending, pervasive voice of the past kept powerfully audible in the present.

THE HIGH COST OF AMNESIA: JEREMIAH 2:1-13

In moving to this text from Deuteronomy 8, we move from sermon to poem, from proclamation to imaginative oracle. What Moses anticipated in Deuteronomy 8, Jeremiah in 2:1-13 can now specify. This is a people which has become prosperous, secure, tenured, beguiled into self-sufficiency. The predictable outcome is that this community has ceased to do its memory work. It thought such work now was, if not silly, at least a choosable elective which it opted not to choose. As the adults ceased to take memory work seriously, the children picked up the conclusion that memory is not important anyway. As a result, everyone, young and old, gave up on the memory.

The poet goes back just a little to let God engage in some pathos-filled remembering (vv. 2-3). God can remember that with which Israel no longer bothers:

> I remember the devotion of your youth,
>   your love as a bride,
> how you followed me in the wilderness,
>   in a land not sown. (v. 2)

This powerful, holy Rememberer can recall good old days, days of a honeymoon in a patriarchal society. Yahweh remembers when Israel was a young bride with passionate love, filled with limitless devotion. The remembered response of "devotion" is *hesed*, complete commitment relying on full mutuality. That love was so deep and unquestioning that Israel followed wherever Yahweh led, and where Yahweh led was into the wilderness, a land not sown, a land not under cultivation. The poem makes direct contact with the preaching of Moses in Deuteronomy 8. The journey of covenant was into the wilderness where your bread was given, your clothes did not wear out, your feet did not swell. We were both so happy. We never had so little or were so happy. Yahweh says, "I remember it, can you? I long for it, do you?"

In v. 5 there comes an abrupt jolt in the poetry: what went wrong? Something is deeply wrong; the good old days are decisively ended. Yahweh speaks as though this terrible ending had happened almost without being noticed. Yahweh says, "I do not know what has happened, but everything has gone sour. Whereas you willingly went after me, now you go far from me, now you go after worthlessness. You have traded me in for something more contemporary, cheap, quick, and trivial." There is a massive crisis in the relationship. Israel has quit on its solemn vows and has gone for new companions that are inherently fickle, and cannot give what Israel needs and wants. Yahweh is genuinely puzzled over the betrayal, the travesty, the humiliation.

Then comes an indictment against Israel (v. 6-8). It is not easy to determine the relationship of v. 5 to vv. 6-8. Perhaps the indictment of vv. 6-8 is the result of v. 5, or maybe it is the other way around. In any case, the central issue is that Israel "did not say" (v. 6). Israel did not say what needed to be said, that which it had always said in times past. Israel did not recite the core memory, did not confess or affirm or teach or enact its constitutive narrative identity.

We do not know why the recital stopped, but Yahweh has now noticed that the recital has indeed stopped. The cessation of the recital is likely a clue to all that has gone wrong, that has eroded this love affair of mutuality.

This is what Israel has been taught to say:

> They did not say, "Where is YHWH
>   who brought us up from the land of Egypt,
> who led us in the wilderness,
>   in a land of deserts and pits,
> in a land of drought and deep darkness,
>   in a land that no one passes through,
>   where no one lives?"
> I brought you into a plentiful land
>   to eat its fruits and its good things.
> But when you entered you defiled my land,
>   and made my heritage an abomination. (vv. 6-7)

The subject of the recital is Yahweh. Yahweh is the "thou," the subject of the great verbs, the initiator of all that is important. Yahweh is the subject of this recital that is dominated by the term *land* — land of Egypt, land of wilderness, land of deserts and pits, land of drought and deep darkness, land with no inhabitants. The whole land is referred to Yahweh.

Israel's memory is all about land — living in the land of oppressors, living in a land without resources. Israel's memory is about Yahweh's will for land, and its discovery that you must have land to live. It is gift land. Thus the recital parallels the preaching of Moses:

> For YHWH your God is bringing you into a good land, a land with flowing streams, with springs and underground waters welling up in valleys and hills, a land of wheat and barley, of vines and fig trees and pomegranates, a land of olive trees and honey, a land where you may eat bread without scarcity, where you will lack nothing. (Deut. 8:7-9)

It is a land of gift.

Then in Jeremiah 2:7, the poetry turns decisively. Now Yahweh speaks in the first person, after the recital and quotation of v. 6. Yahweh remembers that it was precisely Yahweh who enacted the story of the land for Israel;

> I brought you into a plentiful land
> to eat its fruits and its good things.

Yahweh kept the promise of the land. Yahweh gave land, fruit, goodness, blessing. Then follows a harsh adversative:

> But when you entered, you defiled my land,
> and made my heritage an abomination.

Now for the first time in this discussion of the land, Israel is the subject of the verbs. The only verbs Israel gets are "defile," "make abomination." You not only failed to remember; in your amnesia, you rejected the gift of land and fixed it so that the blessed land became a place of curse that could no longer give the gifts God intended. The careless action of Israel has managed to nullify and silence the shaping memory, so that Israel has nothing powerful left to remember. Israel has destroyed its land, and its story that keeps the land defined. Israel is left with the barren land, a burned out land, and an emptied memory, completely without resources.

The leadership is just like the people, filled with neglectful forgetting (v. 8, cf. Hos. 4:9). In v. 8 the leadership is named: priests, handlers of torah, i.e., lawyers, kings, prophets. The critique levied against all of them is that, "They did not say, 'Where is YHWH?'" Thus the two indictments are parallel. Both people (v. 6) and leaders (v. 8) did not say, "Where is YHWH?" i.e., they did not remember and retell the story. They scuttled the memory. They forget, just the way Moses in Deuteronomy 8 had anticipated.

And when they forgot, they forgot the past, they forgot Yahweh, they forgot themselves, their history, their identity, their faith, their vocation, their *raison d'etre*. They went after phony loyalties, false gods, Baal, self-securing religious technology. They created a situation of lies, dishonesty, and denial. They ended up saying to each other, "Peace, peace," when there is no peace (6:14, 8:11). They engaged in incredible, brazen euphemisms in order to keep from seeing the reality of their life (cf. Isa. 5:20).

The outcome of such amnesia is that their wells run dry.[4]

> For my people have committed two evils:
>   they have forsaken me,
> the foundation of living water,
>   and dug out cisterns for themselves,
> cracked cisterns that can hold no water.
>   (Jer. 2:13)

Jerusalem is forced to rely on its own cracked cisterns which guarantee that life in a dry climate is impossible. That is, amnesia leads to death. This poignant poem makes three strong assertions:

- there was indeed a precious season of genuine embrace and loyalty (vv. 2-3);
- there was a long season of forgetting when both people and leadership forget to remember (vv. 4-8); and
- forgetting causes the well to run dry, and life to shrivel up (vv. 9-13).

These two powerful texts, Deuteronomy 8 and Jeremiah 2, need to be seen together. In Deuteronomy 8, Moses warns that affluence and self-sufficiency lead to amnesia which leads to perishing. Jeremiah 2 brings the threats of Deuteronomy 8 to fruition. There has been a forgetting, and now there will be a shriveling unto death.

All of this rhetoric, of course, is poetry and metaphor of a daring kind. It is not simply historical description and political analysis. These poems of advocacy and statements of emergency nonetheless match the historical outcome of the city of Jerusalem. The poets had it right. As you know, as Moses anticipated and Jeremiah warned, the city of forgetting came to a terrible crisis. Invasion, destruction, deportation, and displacement followed. Jews were either taken from their homeland into the suffering and dismay of exile,[5] or they were left bereft in their homeland with the human infrastructure of the city completely destroyed. Either way, Jews ended in a deathliness. Remarkably, the Bible is consistent in asserting that this terrible ending is not to be explained by Babylonian expansionism, or by poor political leadership in Jerusalem, but by forgetting torah identity. The collapse of Jerusalem is a theological one that is rooted in the loss of memory. (See the same verdict in Hosea 2:13.)

THE STRUGGLE TO REMEMBER: ISAIAH 51:1-3

After the dismay of 587 BCE, when life in Jerusalem was savaged by the exile, Judaism engaged in a deep struggle to reclaim its normative memory. As forgetting produced displacement, so remembering is necessary for recovery and homecoming. In a text some decades after Jeremiah but before Ezra and Nehemiah, the poetry of Isaiah can make this urging:

> Look to the rock from which you were hewn
>> and to the quarry from which you were dug.
> Look to Abraham your father and to Sarah who
>> bore you;
>> for he was but one when I called him,
>> but I blessed him and made him many.
> (Isa. 51:1b-2)

The poem addresses the ones in exile who want to get right with God, i.e., the ones who pursue righteousness and seek Yahweh (cf. v. 1). What they need to do is to recover memory, all the way back to the book of Genesis. Specifically, the memory championed here is the memory of Abraham and Sarah. It is telling indeed that in this particular place, the poetry does not urge a return to Moses and torah, but a recovery of Genesis and promise. Exactly in a season of dismay and despair, it is to these primal parents that reference is made. Remember Abraham and all the old stories of this old man without hope, who dared to argue with God (Gen. 18:22-32), who mocked God's promise (Gen. 17:17), but who also trusted God (Gen. 15:1-6), and who risked his precious son in full obedience (Gen. 22:1-14). Remember Sarah, the mother of our family, barren and helpless, desperate and mocking (Gen. 18:12-15). In the end it is Sarah who laughed the innocent, boisterous laugh of Easter, because God had done for her what God had said would be done (Gen. 21:6-7). Remember miracles, remember impossibilities, remember stories that define reality against conventional possibilities. Remember an account of your life in which holiness is an active force, promise is a palpable agent, and providence is an overriding reality.

Remember, and then shake loose of destructive definitions of reality which are false. The poetry of Isaiah 51 is addressed to exiles caught in the throes of the imperial ideology of Babylon. That ideology had canceled promise with propaganda, had dismissed promise by present satiation, had denied providence by the ruthless claims of imperial power. Remembering is the hard choosing of an alternative present authorized by a subversive past. When that subversive past is given up, an alternative present is rendered completely unavailable. For this poet in exile, then, the choice is heard and told. Choose memory and you get with it a liberated alternative. Choose amnesia and what you will inescapably get is the reductive despair of the empire, which absolutizes the status quo and precludes any imagination of an alternative.

EZRA'S REINCORPORATION

In light of this account of warning, indictment, and appeal we return to Nehemiah 8:

- the *warning* of Deuteronomy 8 is given, that prosperity causes amnesia;
- the *condemnation* of Jeremiah 2 is sounded, noticing that the memory has been abandoned; and
- the *invitation* of Isaiah 51 for a recovery of memory is proclaimed.

We now consider Nehemiah 8 as the focal point of the struggle of Jerusalem for its primal memory. They were all at the meeting, women and men. The entire torah is read, the whole memory renewed by the most authoritative leader of Judaism. Interpretation was given so that the torah could be intelligently appropriated as serious business in a contemporary situation. This is indeed the refounding of Judaism after a long, terrible, destructive season of amnesia. It is as though Jews are here coming out of a coma into a torah-awakening. Upon recovery, one asks, "where am I, who am I, how did this happen?" For Jews, the answers are all in the torah, the story which brings Jews to the moment in their quintessential oddness. I want now to review the poignant response made to this reading and interpretation of the torah by Ezra.

"The people wept" (8:9). We are not told why they wept. Perhaps it was the grief of repentance when they touched their own deep guilt. Perhaps, and I think this is more likely, the weeping was a deep, visceral release of vulnerability and relief, when the long season of denial was finally past, an acknowledgment that our conventional consensus about the world no longer contradicts our own true, core identity. One becomes exhausted by faking it, in the massive pretense of being something other than one really is. When one arrives back home at one's true self, the floodgates of hurt and passion lead to torrents of tears, a mixture of hurt and grief and relief and gratitude, a yearning satisfied, an honest disclosure of self that had seemed impossible. This moment is a candid coming out of the closet as Jews, no longer ashamed or embarrassed by that fundamental self-acknowledgement.

As the empire had long required such denial, I believe there is a pent-up sense in our technological society, pent up so deep in pretense that we ourselves do not discern the power and depth of our yearning for homecoming. It is no wonder that the Jews cried at the cadence of the torah, for it is indeed their *Muttersprache*. In response to this spasm of weeping, the leadership counters with joy. They urge another reading of this moment of torah crisis:

> "This day is holy to YHWH your God; do not mourn or weep." For all the people wept when they heard the words of the torah. Then he said to them, "Go your way, eat the fat and drink the sweet wine and send portions of them to those for whom nothing is prepared, for this day is holy to YHWH; and do not be grieved, for the joy of YHWH is your strength." So the Levites stilled all the people, saying, "Be quiet, for this day is holy; do not be grieved." And all the people went their way to eat and drink and to send portions and to make great rejoicing, because they had understood the words that were declared to them. (vv. 9-12)

It is a day of complete joy. The ground and power of *joy* is the same as the ground and power of *weeping*. These are two elemental responses to the same crisis. This joy is rooted in the reliable rule and reality of Yahweh. Verse 12 concludes with a telling judgment: The reason for utter joy is "that they had understood the words declared to them." They understood, as they had not in their long season of amnesia, what it meant to belong to Yahweh, worker of miracles, actor for freedom, giver of commandments. Their joy is a genuine theological homecoming, for Jews were now finally, in their true homecoming, coming down where they ought to be. The raw responses of grief and joy are intimately connected; both break the dam of denial, both open the flood-gates of a most elemental homecoming.

As they studied the torah, they found as a primal point of teaching the Festival of Booths (vv. 13-18). This great sacramental act was a physical, bodily, visible reengagement with a peculiar past. The festival is a reappropriation of a very old, defining memory. In obedience to the urging of Moses himself, they were commanded:

> That they should publish and proclaim in all their
> towns and in Jerusalem as follows, "Go out to the
> hills and bring branches of olive, wild olive, myrtle,
> palm, and other leafy trees to make booths, as it is
> written."

And they did (v. 16). For seven days, they made and lived in booths. They experienced the fragility, the precariousness, and vulnerability of their true Jewishness. They lived amidst the presence of old mothers and fathers who had departed the empire long ago. They communed with those parents who entered the wilderness, lived exposed, and found Yahweh's fidelity to be adequate. They disengaged from the old demanding supports of the Egyptian empire (Exodus), and in the same moment, they disengaged from the demanding supports of the contemporary Babylonian and then Persian empires (exile). They submitted themselves to the costs and risks and joys that belong to this memory. They could sense in their bodies distance from that very affluence that had placed them in the crisis in the first place. That is, a return to a circumstance of *vulnerability* shook them loose from their *self-sufficiency*.

There is something very odd about the Festival of Booths. On the one hand, it is an experience of *exposed homelessness*. Indeed, in Atlanta, The Open Door, a powerful witness on behalf of the homeless, calls this "the festival of homelessness," and invites fully housed people to submit for a period to the threat of living in exposed booths. It really is an act of leaving our conventional securities. On the other hand, and at the same time, this festival is evidence of *true homefulness*, when Israel senses that this is the right, safe place, lived with the sojourning God who keeps God's people safe, even in dangerous exposure. Thus the festival of *homelessness* turns out to be true *homefulness*.

This festival at the same poignant moment is homelessness and homefulness, exposure and guarantee, and in its practice, the people around Ezra touched their true, long-forgotten identity. The text says both that there was a "solemn assembly," and also "great rejoicing." Moreover, day by day, Ezra read the torah, embracing the memory, receiving the past, situating Israel in its true locus.

In the disciplines of fasting and sackcloth, the Israelites "separated themselves from all foreigners" and confessed their sin (9:1-2). This act in the drama needs to be understood carefully. Wrongly understood, according to Christian stereotypes of Jews, this separation sounds like arrogant legalism. Such a view misses the point completely. Rather, this community in its amnesia had assimilated itself, domesticated its memory, and compromised its identity, so that it had nothing left of itself. Judaism had become such a detrimental embarrassment, that Jews had worked to overcome their Jewishness. And now, in these dangerous liturgical acts, Jews are facing up to their oddity, to their strong commitment, to their distinctive obedience. The recovery of distinctiveness entails the acceptance of an odd identity. I report this point to you because I believe the church in the United States faces a crisis of accommodation and compromise that is near to final evaporation.[6] Note well, the distinctiveness is not in doctrine or in morality, but in memory. For the text adds that all through this time of separation, "They stood up in their place and read from the book of the law" (9:3).

Then follows a long prayer by Ezra (9:6-37). It is a remarkable prayer, paralleled to some extent by prayers in Ezra 9 and Daniel 9. The reading of the torah, entering the booths, and asserting oddity through separateness drive Jerusalem to prayer. I will make only three comments about this long and rich prayer.

First, the prayer is a long, careful recital of Jewish history, i.e., the prayer itself is an exercise in remembering. Prayer is not always present-tense immediacy. The primary prayer we have like it in our liturgical practice is the extensive Eucharistic prayer which serves to locate the sacrament amidst "prophets and apostles, martyrs and saints." Prayer is a place in which the beloved community is surrounded by all our ancestors in faith.

Second, the prayer is an honest acknowledgment that this long history is a tale of recalcitrance, disobedience, and sin. From the beginning, Israel had such a difficult time trusting and obeying, and the present generation understands itself as a part of that sorry resistance to the purposes of Yahweh.

Third, the prayer is not, however, an act of groveling and brow-beating. The primary tone of the prayer is doxological, in which the wondrous generosity of God powerfully overrides the long-term failure of Israel. It is thus not only a petition for God's mercy, but a bold, confident trust in God's mercy as the ultimate reality for the future. What Israel finally heard in torah through the tutelage of Ezra is that Israel is held firmly in the mercy of God. Thus the reading of the torah evokes this prayer of trust. Torah drives to prayer.

Such trust in God's goodness is the decisive oddity of Jewishness. This oddity of mercy heard in the torah and known in the booths makes Jews free of imperial necessity, conformity, and docility, freed for joyous obedience to Yahweh in the world.

This great liturgy culminates in a solemn covenant (9:38) which the NRSV calls a "firm agreement." The liturgy is a process of covenant renewal whereby Jews gladly assent to their distinctive identity, rooted in mercy and enacted as obedience. The liturgy schools Jews in an odd identity. As they accept again this odd identity, they are freed from any generic identity as citizens of the Persian empire. Thus I suggest a powerful correlation between *forgetting* and the outcome of *accommodation and compromise* to dominant cultural values, and *remembering* as the source of *courage, energy, and freedom* for God's will in a world organized to resist God's will.

This fresh oath to share in covenant leads in chapter 10 to a series of decisions designed to enhance community. This includes an oath to follow torah (10:29), a practice of the sabbath (10:31), and solemn pledges of money (10:32-39). The recovery of identity leads to discipline and to generosity. That generosity extends, as noted in 8:10, to sharing with those for whom "nothing has been prepared." This identity empowers Jews to reach well beyond themselves to those who have less than they do. Identity culminates in an act of generosity which cannot be undertaken by those without secure identity.

OUR FORGETTING AND REMEMBERING

My theme is that forgetters can become rememberers. My thesis is that evangelism is a task not simply of making outsiders into insiders, but of summoning insiders from amnesia to memory. I suspect that very many so-called insiders are in fact functional outsiders, "alienated from the commonwealth of Israel," i.e., completely cut off from the odd identity of covenant. And as outsiders are invited by Joshua to embrace this textual rendering of reality, so dysfunctional insiders are at a crisis of being retextualized by Ezra as functional, intentional, participating insiders.

I believe that the reality of amnesia is massive among us. That amnesia (which on the surface shows up as "illiteracy") causes the church to lack in any serious missional energy. It is only this odd memory, operative at the pre-rational places in our life, that gives energy for social action, generosity in stewardship, freedom for worship, courage in care for outsiders, and passion for God's promises. Without memory, there will be little of courage, generosity, freedom, or passion.

I want then to reflect on this deep amnesia in the church. Taken at the most formal level, it is worth acknowledging that modernity, i.e., the large intellectual environment of the Enlightenment in which we all have been nurtured, is programmatically aimed against tradition. That is, the rise of modern consciousness which brought with it scientific thinking, emancipation of the human spirit, and the emergence of the social sciences, viewed tradition as essentially authoritarian, detrimental restraint. As freedom became the watchword of modernity, so tradition, rootage, and memory became the enemies of maturity and emancipation.

Most of us have not thought systematically about the Enlightenment. Most of us simply went to college, found new emancipation, and found our religious upbringing to be an awkward embarrassment. Then, in the midst of that embarrassment when there have been attempts to reenter the memory, the memory has been skewed, weakened, and trivialized in terms of closed moralism or obscurantism. We have arrived at a great divide between those who have "outgrown" the old memory, either to a kind of urbane liberalism based in current experience, or a spirit-filled

piety that finds everything present tense, or a mean-spirited tradi-
tionalism that is judgmental and restrictive, but lacks the characteristically expansive polyvalence of our Jewish memory.

Very many of us, as products of amnesia, can recall a pivot
point where the memory was powerfully available. More conservative people can name the time and place of appropriation, i.e., of
"being saved," but the saving is often so immediate and private that
it does not amount to much of an appropriation. My own pivot
point in my evangelical tradition was not overly intense or pious.
I do, nonetheless, remember that day. The oath was that lyrical,
doxological, wondrous last answer to the *Evangelical Catechism*. It
ends with this sweeping, mind-boggling vow:

> Lord Jesus, for thee I live, for thee I suffer, for thee
> I die! Lord Jesus, thine will I be in life and death!
> Grant me, O Lord, eternal salvation! Amen.

A friend of mine and I took that vow in our thirteenth year. And
then we were ushered into the sacristy of the St. Paul's Church by
Mr. Chester Grube, and we signed the book. It was a moment in
which we felt our names were being written in the Book of Life!

For many people since that pivotal moment, in the face of vows
taken, life has been mostly progressive amnesia. The amnesia is a
lack of growth, so that the memory does not keep pace with the
adult growth in many other areas of life. Many are left with no
memory, or with a truncated, childish memory that has almost no
credibility in the dangerous world of adulthood.

I propose in such a situation, that Nehemiah 8 is a model for
evangelical activity. We do indeed forget in our affluence. We are
talked out of our memory. We do in fact forget to recite. We also
live in an environment of a hostile culture where the fabric of faith
is thin and fragile. We are at a moment of recovering a lost
inheritance. That recovery now requires reading, interpretation,
boothing, appropriation of the whole memory.

Nehemiah 8 is a moment of incredible and powerful liminality
for this community, when old patterns have failed, when people in
their vulnerability of grief and joy could for an instant leave their
conventional home and live in the booths of fragility, in the
presence of many ancestors, prepared to be reconfigured and

reidentified. Such a "re-boothing" of the imagination cannot be done in the company of careless, indifferent, or hostile outsiders. "Re-boothing" requires an embrace of our distinctiveness, expressed in prayer, the sabbath, vows, tithes, and oaths.

Ezra did not worry about the Persians. His first thought was the recovery of odd community. Because he knew that this identity was the will of "maker of heaven and earth," he believed that the most important thing he could do in praise of heaven and in obedience on earth was to recover this odd community that refused the generic identity of the empire. Given such an odd identity, it is no wonder the people dissolved in grief and joy, for what had been jettisoned was now regiven and reclaimed. These belated children of the torah could still remember that there was bread given, that our clothes did not wear out, that our feet did not swell. They could remember the long story of gracious mercy as still definitional now, present tense, in and against and beyond the empire.

The petition with which Ezra ends his prayer is candid:

> Here we are, slaves to this day — slaves in the land
> that you gave to our ancestors to enjoy its fruit and
> its good gifts. Its rich yield goes to the kings whom
> you have set over us because of our sins; they have
> power also over our bodies and over our livestock
> at their pleasure, and we are in great distress.
> (9:36-37)

That candid prayer is matched by Ezra's invitation to bold doxology:

> Stand up and bless YHWH your God from everlast-
> ing to everlasting. Blessed be your glorious name,
> which is exalted above all blessing and praise. (9:5)

Both petition and praise are acts of liberated oddity arising in the resolve to keep the covenant:

> Because of all this we make a firm agreement in
> writing, and on that sealed document are inscribed

92

the names of our officials, our Levites, and our priests. (9:38)

We are relearning through such a text and such a posture what it means to have our names inscribed in such a "firm agreement."

Beloved Children Become Belief-ful Adults[1]

Thus far we have identified two candidates for evangelism, and for each we have identified a definitional meeting for the evangelizing process. For outsiders, we have found in Joshua 24 a meeting whereby *outsiders become insiders*. For adults within the community of faith, we have found in Nehemiah 8 a meeting whereby *members are "re-tented"* into the passionate vision of risk and vulnerability that is decisive for the community.

We come now to the third candidate for evangelism, namely, the children of believers who may or may not grow up to become "consenting adults."[2] Here the matter of evangelism is more complex and more difficult than it is in the other cases. Both from the text itself, and from our own experience with our own children as believers, it is clear that there is no single, decisive meeting which will suit such children, for nurture and incorporation are not so easy with our children.[3] Nurture and incorporation require not a one-time meeting, but an ongoing conversation, whereby the children-en-route-to-adult begins, a little at a time at one's own pace, to affirm and claim the "news" which defines the community.

The process of growing into adulthood is inscrutable, given the dialectic of freedom and independence, the requirement of individuation, and the indispensability of embedment in the community. This conversation, unlike the previously cited meetings, is never done with. It goes on and on. Indeed, I share the view that the conversation never reaches a fixed, finished conclusion, for the conversation itself is the very reality of evangelism.

The taxing work of this conversation is a primary enterprise of the community. It follows that the tortured route of growth in faith cannot be hurried or preempted. For that reason, the conversation is at some points adult testimony and advocacy, a readiness to speak plainly and passionately about our own believing heart and mind. At other times, the conversation requires the adult community to be present in accepting, receiving ways to provide context, courage, and energy for the probing which may (or may not) lead to commitment and membership. As every parent will attest, it is exceedingly difficult to maintain an effective pattern of advocacy and receptivity. For some of us, advocacy becomes all, and is experienced by our young as excessively authoritarian. (This is the characteristic temptation of militant, so-called evangelicals.) For some of us, receptivity becomes all, and is experienced by our young as excessively passive, cowardly, noncommittal abdication. (This is the characteristic temptation of communities overly committed to the "therapeutic" and to "active listening.") There is of course no right way; either way, in an authoritarian or abdicating mode, we shall finish the conversation with some regret. The wonder of course is that sometimes our advocacy is recalled by our children with gratitude, and sometimes our receptivity is acknowledged as healing. Faith does on occasion arise, partly because of us, partly in spite of us.

BEING WITH AND FOR OUR CHILDREN

It can easily be asserted that the situation of children and young people at the end of the twentieth century is a peculiarly problematic one. It is more difficult, more demanding, and more dangerous to grow up now than in any time in our recent past. The situation of our young is peculiar and complex because (a) there are so many choices with so much freedom, generated by the advances of technology and the communication revolutions; (b) there is a large failure of reliable values and social structures, caused by the end of the Euro-American hegemony; and (c) there is a heightened self-consciousness and self-awareness of young persons, as the demands and options of post-modern life are immediately available and unavoidable.

One of the results of this manifold revolution of culture is the disappearance of a benign alliance between faith and culture which has been for so long taken for granted among us. That is, in the U.S. culture with its dominant and well-established Protestant (mostly Calvinist) values, it was relatively easy and obvious to take faith along with the rest of the package of viable community, functioning family, and a due sense of "America's" preeminence and priority in the world. It was easy, natural, and unquestioned to grow up "well-placed" in the world, without excessive doubt and with reasonable confidence in the continuity of faith and culture into the foreseeable future. It was "natural" and not problematic to inherit and appropriate some semblance of faith.

It is a disturbing truism to say that such a benign alliance is no longer available. The reasons for that fissure in our cultural experience are complex, and perhaps not fully understood by us. The elements in that fissure certainly include the Vietnam War and the Civil Rights movement which irreversibly altered public discourse in the United States. The rise of third world power and culture (and Islam) has rightly produced a failure of nerve about our presumed preeminence in the world. As the "center" has been under assault, so our conventional supports of faith and culture have yielded to a deep anxiety about our place in the world. This in turn has produced brutality in defense of our place, and greed as the pursuit of at least our share. Instead of a benign alliance, we find ourselves in a conflictual situation of assault and defense. We tend to cope by numbed withdrawal into an individualism which refuses to notice.[4] The numbed refusal to notice of course has its religious dimensions, but it is a religious dimension that only by great distortion can be regarded as Christian.

I have come to wonder then if faith, as we adults have known it, is any more available for our young, and if so on what terms. I have the impression that our young are mostly confronted by two options. On the one hand, our young, like ourselves, are seduced into a comfortable, seductive modernism that makes all the sounds of humanness, but never in fact keeps its promise. That is, there is a youth culture that has learned to pay the right kind of lip service, but along with the lip service has adopted a rather comfortable, self-indulgent individualism.

On the other hand, to break with such seductive secularism, enormous intentionality is required within a sustaining community of support. The form of this intentionality and support characteristically is a highly moralistic community that is essentially turned in upon personal and "family" values with intense certitude, matched by a disregard for the large culture that impinges upon that community. I think particularly of student groups in university settings, which do the best they can, surrounded by a militantly secular culture which leaves serious faith essentially dislocated and contextless.

As we ponder a conversation with our young, we may wonder if secularized, self-serving indifference and legalistic individualism are the only options. We may wonder if a more public faith, a faith which takes a larger, critical view of culture is possible, and if with a larger public view, buoyancy for discipleship as citizens is a possibility. Speaking quite concretely and practically, I wonder if faith as we have known it is now even possible for our young. I should want to argue that insofar as our young are practitioners of secular indifference, or adherents to legalistic individualism, they are candidates for an evangelical conversation. I am not sure what such a conversation might entail, but three matters seem to be evident:

The conversation must take place in a context of *unconditional advocacy*. This advocacy is not for certain "positions," but for the worth, value, future, and very existence of the young persons. The young need adults who are quite literally "crazy" for them.[5] This point is so obvious that we forget it. We are speaking here of a conversation that mediates free grace. This unconditional advocacy is increasingly difficult in a market economy where everything and everyone has commodity value, and in which scarcity of goods drives us anxiously to value merit, competence, and productivity. The conversation itself, as advocacy and as receptivity, is a means of grace, but we adults are less and less prone to such conversation, much preferring for ourselves a production-oriented mode of living, in which even our children take on instrumental value.

Young people need someone who is "crazy" about them. Alongside that affirmative *sine qua non*, however, perhaps at a later "stage," a young person must have a coherent construct of reality, so that all the parts make sense as a whole. That is, there is a cognitive, intellectual dimension to faith that needs articulation. The conversation with our young must be persistently interpretive. The act of interpretation need not be excessively didactic, but simply ongoing readiness to help connect the little pieces to a larger context to which the adult community of faith subscribes.

My impression is that this interpretive capacity is presently weak and neglected in the adult church, partly because many adults themselves do not have any live sense of a coherent faith. The articulation of faith as a substantive body of teaching is at present exceedingly *ad hoc* in the church, as we move from one emergency to the next. The outcome of such an *ad hoc* approach is that the bits and pieces, i.e., the familiar formulae of faith, are inadvertently put together according to some other ideology, by the claims of secular individualism, free market conviction, or a frightened legalism, so that the parts are distorted by the context in which they are placed.

The coherent construal of reality through faith must of course give a place to the individual with unconditional advocacy. That indispensable focus upon the individual, however, must be matched by a larger cosmic claim. The God "who loves you" is none other than the "maker of heaven and earth," who "makes poor and makes rich."

Acts of unconditional advocacy and of a larger construal of reality require that the evangelical *conversation with our young be profoundly and intentionally "counter-nurture."* That is, the purpose of the conversation is not that our young would become "good Americans" or "moral" or "productive," any one of which may or may not be desirable. It is rather that our young should be able to perceive, embrace, and enact the world according to the peculiar memory and vision of faith held by the gospel community. Quite explicitly I propose that this conversation should echo the ditty of Sesame Street which affirms that "This one is not like the others." Conversion to Christian faith is a conversion to oddity in the world, odd over against secular self-indulgence, odd over against legalistic communalism and market individualism.

Thus I concur that our situation vis à vis our children is nearly unprecedented. The convergence of cultural options, dangers, and resources is like none that has ever existed. At the same time, however, I suggest that the elements of *unconditional advocacy*, *coherent construal*, and *counter-nurture* are not unknown in our community. Indeed these are the recurring staples of conversation in this community, whose young have always been at risk. The reason the young in this community are at risk is because this faith is scandalous and radical, and cannot simply be passed on. It must be reappropriated, and this is done afresh and in new ways in each generation. I do not imagine that in our place we can do that work the way others have done it before. But I also imagine we can learn from them. Thus I propose to ask, even in our unprecedented situation, how did our ancestors conduct the conversation? Here I will review a series of texts which shows this community involved in an ongoing conversation with its young, who turn out to be our young.

TESTIMONIAL ANSWERS

We begin our study of the conversation with six texts which voice the innocent curiosity of the children who wonder about and want in on the sacramental mysteries of their parents.[6] This aspect of the conversation leads to *direct, unembarrassed testimony done by the adult community with certitude and urgency*. The questions of the children arise because the parents are engaged in liturgical acts of obedience. Indeed, it may be that part of the reason for the liturgical act is precisely to evoke the child's question. In any case, the texts of Moses and Joshua fully anticipate that right worship is linked to a definitional memory:

- Exodus 12:29 — passover: "struck down" the Egyptians.
- Exodus 13:8 — unleavened bread: "did for me."
- Exodus 13:14 — offer of the first born: "brought us out of Egypt."

- Deuteronomy 6:21 — ordinances: "brought us out of Egypt."
- Joshua 4:7 — placement of stones: "the waters . . . were cut off."
- Joshua 4:21 — placement of stones: "Israel crossed over . . . on dry ground."

These six exchanges, while they are very different in a variety of details, constitute a special corpus of material designed for intergenerational conversation.[7] In each of the six cases, the adult community is engaged in a liturgical act, the meaning of which is hidden and, judged by a neutral observer, irrational. Indeed, the content of the act in each case is to penetrate behind obvious rationality, for the warrant for this community is grounded in memories which precede any conventional rationality.

The liturgical act, which betokens a sacramental sense of existence, is respectively passover (Exod. 12:26), unleavened bread (Exod. 13:8), sacrifice of the first-born (Exod. 13:14), the observance of ordinances (Deut. 6:20), and the placement of stones (Josh. 4:6, 21). In each case, the act is an odd act. It is not something that everyone does, nor is it something that on the face of it is self-evident. It is an act that would only be done by those who accept that this odd act continues with enduring sacramental power into the present. The liturgical, sacramental act is Israel's most explicit act of counter-nurture. It asserts that there is something here which is more than and other than meets the eye.

In each case (with a partial exception in Exod. 13:8), the sacramental act of loyalty evokes a child's question:

- What do you mean by this observance (Exod. 12:26)?
- What does this mean (Exod. 13:14)?
- What is the meaning of the decree, and the statutes, and the ordinances that YHWH our God has commanded you (Deut. 6:20)?
- What do those stones mean to you (Josh. 4:6)?
- What do these stones mean (Josh. 4:21)?

The question is innocent, as children are wont to be, only wanting to share the mystery. It is telling that in some of these texts, the question is objective: "What is this?" In some others, however, the question is quite personal and existential: "What is this *to you?*" The child asks not about the celebration, but about the parent. It is as though the child asks, "Who are you, what are you up to, why does it matter to you?" In truth, the stones and festivals have no "objective" meaning. They are only confessional constructs that are signs and witnesses. That is, the child in innocence is prepared to accept that the pivotal meanings of the community are sacramental.

The answers given by the parents to the questions of the children move immediately away from the sign to the miracle signified:

- YHWH passed over the houses of the Israelites in Egypt, when he struck down the Egyptians but spared our houses (Exod. 12:27).
- YHWH did for me when I came out of Egypt (Exod. 13:8).
- By strength of hand YHWH brought us out of Egypt. . . YHWH killed all the first-born" (13:14-15).
- YHWH brought us out of Egypt with a mighty hand. YHWH displayed before our eyes great and awesome signs and wonders (Deut. 6:21-22).
- The waters of the Jordan were cut off (Josh. 4:6).
- YHWH your God dried up the waters (Josh. 4:23).

In each case, the parental answer witnesses the miracle. The telling of the miracle invokes a powerful active verb (in 4:6 passive), and the naming of Yahweh as the agent of the verb. Thus the parental response moves immediately and majestically from the visible object to the named miracle and the name of the miracle worker. The conversation attests that the life, identity, and vocation of this community is rooted in a quite concrete miracle, that can only be attested sacramentally.

It is this recital of miracle and miracle worker that provides the substance and mode of counter-nurture. The point of counter-nurture is that the world is not as it seems. The powers that seem to be in charge, the ideology that seems compelling, the requirements that seem non-negotiable, are all penultimate. They are endlessly subverted and destabilized by these wonders that endure in their authority.[8]

In a shrewd study of Deuteronomy 6:20-25, Michael Fishbane has observed that in this text, the son asks the question, "What is the meaning of the commandments which Yahweh has commanded *you*."[9] The answer of the parent is, "*We* were slaves." The difference in pronouns is telling. The question means to put distance between the generations. The "wonder" celebrated belongs to the parents, but it is not claimed or appropriated by the questioning son. The answer of the parent, by contrast, refuses the distance, and wants to extend the claim of the miracle so that it includes the child into a more comprehensive *us*. Thus Fishbane observes that this exchange of question and answer exemplifies the problem of parents and children. The parents intend that all generations are contemporaries and participants, but the children posture themselves as "distemporaries."[10] This is a recurring problem between the generations.

The strategy of the parent is important. The parent does not insist or coerce or assume too much. The parent continues instead to make the witness inclusive, choosing to ignore the son's distancing, and proceeding on the affirmation that the miracle is for "us." The parent does not argue or insist, but refuses the distance, permitting the son to claim it, even while declining to speak in those categories. It is likely that the parent's insistence will prevail with the son only if and when the son has a personal experience which gives vitality to the category of miracle. Fishbane proposes that in Joshua 4:6, 21, the Exodus witness is claimed by the later generation of the conquest, which is now able to testify that the miracle has been reenacted (replicated) in a second parallel miracle. Thus the children are permitted to follow at a distance, having the category "miracle" in readiness for the time when experience permits its use. Clearly the children will not have faithfully understood the "conquest," had they not had the Exodus witness ready at hand.

We may wonder about the age of the child who is to ask the question. It is easiest to imagine it is a small child who speaks in innocence. We have a more difficult context if the question is from an older child. Yet, in a community where the conversation has been kept alive, the question continues to recur, perhaps muted, perhaps disguised. I have no doubt that even in distancing resistance or hostility, the faith-categories of the parents persist, so that children and young people of every age are haunted by "miracle," even when a wonder is explained otherwise, even when the awesome name of the miracle worker is seldom uttered. Everything depends upon the capacity of the parents to bear witness in bold ways, to claim for themselves that this memory is indeed a counter memory. Such confidence refuses to "explain" the original miracle more "sensibly," but also refuses to deny the original miracle. Such a parent insists that in a world of real danger and raw power this community, most visibly in its sacramental moment, continues to draw its life from a miracle which summons to obedience.

NARRATIVES OF SATURATION

The miracle kept daily visible and concrete requires *endless and imaginative reiteration* in order to evoke *a response of loyalty*. Perhaps the pivotal passage in this intergenerational communication is Deuteronomy 6:4-9.[11] The visible part of the command of Moses is as "sign" in the hand, as "emblem" on the forehead, and as "writing" on the door post. The sign, emblem, and writing seem rather primitive. But Deuteronomy, a theological pedagogy forged in an emergency, understood very well that explicit signing is a way of keeping oddity available. The sign is aimed at the insiders who are kept daily aware. The sign is not an act of nerve in the presence of outsiders. The family is not embarrassed about its visible oddity.

The visible signs, however, are subordinated in the rhetoric of Deuteronomy to the actual, out-loud recital. The verb "recite" (*shinnen*) means to repeat, reiterate, say again. What is "signed" in vv. 8-9 is sounded in v. 4-5. What is to be reiterated are the words of Israel's most elemental faith affirmation. The recital is *saturation witness*, the real subject of every conversation. It is a conversation that is to be continued *everywhere*, *always*, when at home, when on the road, in lying down, in getting up, i.e., evening and morning, bracketing all the times. The same sorts of verbs are used in Judges 5:10-11:

> Tell of it, you who ride on white donkeys, you who
> sit on new carpets and you who walk by the way. To
> the sound of musicians at the watering places, there
> they repeat the triumphs of YHWH, the triumphs
> of his peasantry in Israel.

Judges 5:10-11 pictures daily gossip at the village well or watering place. The subject of the "gossip" is the same as in all the answers we have considered above. The subject is the transformational miracle of Yahweh which has made life possible, even for these powerless peasants.

This saturation witness of Deuteronomy 6:4-9 which is signed and sounded, has as its subject Yahweh, Yahweh your God, Yahweh alone, Yahweh only, one Yahweh. In this reiterated witness, the subject matter is shifted from "us" and all our getting and spending, all our fears and hopes, to place at the center of the purview of this family the one known as liberator and commander. The governing imperative of Deuteronomy 6:4-11 is that this Yahweh, who is the key actor of the saving story, is the one to love, trust in, fear, honor, hope for, and count on. The pedagogy of saturation intends that the whole of one's life is to be devoted in trust and fidelity of this one and to none other. Thus the oddity of this community, the focus of its counter-nurture, is not its morality or conduct or "values," but this one to whom loyalty is directed, the doer of miracles who makes life possible. This focus on Yahweh speaks against a reticent liberalism which does not want to name the miracle worker; it also speaks against a militant conservatism that wants to reduce life to a set of rules. The imperative to love names the miracle worker, but lets love (loyalty) work its own way through the body of the reciter.

We may pause over the word "recite" (reiterate) in v. 7. Taken at first appearance, the set formula in vv. 4-5 may sound like a recurring mantra. If we consider the whole of the book of Deuteronomy, however, we see that the verb "reiterate" is to be taken with enormous imaginative, interpretive freedom. That is, the evangelist in the conversation must be a skillful, sensitive, hermeneutist. The book of Deuteronomy is not committed to or limited by a repetitive formula. I suggest "recite" means to show the ways in which Yahweh and love of Yahweh appear and emerge in the life of the believing child. The adult community must be prepared to witness to the ways in which the love of Yahweh, the miracle worker, is germane to life in every stage and every circumstance. The creedal formula is only the point of origin for our interpretive tradition which believes there is no conversation in which the sovereignty of Yahweh and devotion to Yahweh are not definitional, against every rival claim. The child is permitted to reimagine and reconstrue his or her life in the presence of Yahweh, a known character in this family.

This community which is concerned to include the next generation in its faith and its passion, worries a lot about getting the power of faith safely entrusted to its young. The worry about this matter is not unlike the way a wealthy family worries about its wealth. On the one hand, it must keep the estate intact. On the other hand, it must have trustworthy children who will responsibly receive and preserve the inheritance. The didactic tradition we have thus far cited in Deuteronomy (and the related texts in Exodus and Joshua) tends to be explicit and direct about this anxiety. Its tone is urgent, and I imagine that it comes through as coercive to the young. To do saturation education may not be the most effective way to work at the problem of intergenerational continuity, and may in the end be counter-productive and self-defeating. As an alternative and corrective to that didactic tradition, I want now to consider a very different set of texts which acknowledge that there is something hidden, inscrutable, and uncanny about this transmission which is beyond the control and management of the adult community.

The ancestral stories in the book of Genesis, in contrast to the Moses-Joshua texts, concern the blessing of God (Gen. 12-50). The blessing is the life-force, the capacity for life that has been promised to and implanted in this community. The witness of the narratives of Genesis 12-50 is that this family of Abraham and Sarah is the peculiar carrier of God's blessing in a world burdened with curse.[12] This means that this family has been entrusted with the power for life that persists even against enormous odds. If we are to translate this claim of blessing into more familiar categories, we may say that there is ordained in this family a kind of buoyancy

105

and affirmation of life that refuses to accept the defeats of history or the finality of death. This same buoyancy and affirmation is what believing parents hope for in their children.

These stories involve a healthy embrace of the self as a carrier of liberated, responsible life which can continue to function effectively against enormous odds. The book of Genesis has as its *leitmotif* the affirmation that "The force is with you." It is this "force" of life given by God that we may transmit to our children. Note well that Genesis, unlike Deuteronomy, is not didactic about this issue, and is not explicit about how such transmission can be done. The narrative of Genesis does not want to transmit teaching (as does Deuteronomy), as much as it wants to pass along the force of Yahweh, i.e. the blessing.

In the ancestral stories, primary focus is repeatedly placed upon the break points between the generations. The stories concern not so much having the blessing as in getting the blessing safely situated in the next generation. Each father and mother are preoccupied with this task, each child waits in eagerness to belong in this special way. In each cycle of the Genesis material, the issue is the same. The stories are told and retold, in order that fathers and mothers, sons and daughters, may learn that the blessing is not theirs to control and assign, but finally the blessing works its own inscrutable way in and through the family.

The Abraham-Sarah story is preoccupied with the yearning for a son (Gen. 12:1–25:18). Sarah is barren and Abraham is old. The presence of Hagar yields a son, but that son is not the child of promise.[13] The promised heir, Isaac, the one who is to carry the blessing, is given only belatedly, by God's wondrous decree. Moreover, this son given only belatedly (21:1-7) is immediately "required" as the test of faith (22:1-14). Even when given, the son does not "belong" to Abraham and Sarah. It is not until the end of the story — after mother Sarah is dead (23:1-20), after Rebekah his wife is located (24:1-67), and after father Abraham is dead (25:1-10) — that Isaac receives the promise (26:2-5). He did not receive the promise as a child. He received the promise only after his own children were born (25:21-26), and after he himself was placed into a crisis by famine (26:1).

It is in that moment that Yahweh finally comes to Isaac and

pronounces this wondrous blessing (26:2-5). Now Isaac receives the promise already made to father Abraham. Now Isaac becomes the focus of the oath, and is assured of children and heirs of his own. That promised blessing, however, is given exactly because father Abraham has been obedient (26:5). The "force" now surges within Isaac into the next generation.

By chapter 27, the blessing is again in crisis. Now Isaac is old and he must see that the blessing is given to his sons. This time the crisis is not finally barrenness (but cf. 25:21), but dispute, a dispute destined before the birth of the sons (25:33). The dispute operates at the very center of the family, with each parent, mother and father, preferring a special son, Jacob or Esau. In the moving narrative of chapter 27, two matters strike us. On the one hand, the blessing is secured by deception (theft) (27:18-29). On the other hand, the bestowal of the blessing is irreversible, leaving the father in deep pathos (27:35-38).

When the story is read in relation to real life, we can see that it is not remote from real families as we know them. Families are like that, and children are like that. The "wave of the future" does not always settle where it ought or where it is intentionally assigned; there are sons and daughters who seize the future of the family and claim it as their own. The outcome is sometimes not what any parent wishes, but it becomes nonetheless a way for the family into the future. Jacob's stealth, Rebekah's cunning, and Isaac's pathos are all in the end a tale of passing the blessing awkwardly but powerfully into the next generation. As it turns out, Jacob becomes a powerful carrier of the promise, one who is prepared to work the promise to its full potential and advantage. Indeed Jacob receives a wondrous promise from God, including that "I will be with you" (28:15, cf. 26:3). Unlike his father, Isaac, who accepts the promise passively, Jacob wants even more. He speaks back to God a condition for obedience which in fact makes a demand of God (28:20-22).

In the third generation of the blessing, as with Sarah and with Rebekah, the problem is barrenness (29:31). The long story of barrenness and blessing is told in order to assert that at no point is there ease in transmission of the promise. Getting the blessing into the next generation is each time problematic. The problem of that transmission dominates the Genesis material. In this instant, the crisis of blessing is magnified by the dream of Joseph (37:5-11). The dream comes uninvited to disrupt the family, as dreams always do. Joseph the younger brother is the beloved son (37:3). His dream seeks to work his special status to the fullest. Again the family is plunged into crisis, for his brothers, the rightful heirs, sense immediately the threat of this spoiled, beloved child.

This story concerning the blessing is odd on two counts. First, nowhere does Joseph formally receive the blessing as have Isaac and Jacob before him. He has dreamed a blessed future and then discerned it (45:1-8), but that is all. He has found the blessing operating in his life without his intention. Second, when father Jacob is old and the blessing is in jeopardy, Joseph takes deliberate steps to secure the blessing for his sons (48:1-20). Remarkably, in this instant, the blessing skips a generation with Joseph being passed over. The narrator is quite explicit about this arrangement (48:5-6). As in chapter 27, moreover, the blessing is wrongly assigned in chapter 48. This time it is done not by deception but as a mistake that is nowhere explained (v. 14). As with Jacob, so now, the younger son Ephraim receives the primary blessing. The mistake, however, is irreversible, and Ephraim is the carrier of blessing into the next generation.

These Genesis stories haunt us, parents and children, not because we take them as "factual." Clearly they are of a very different genre from those in the Exodus-Joshua recitals. These stories belong to the most remote part of our communal memory. In them, however, it is already clear that the story contains an inscrutable dimension which is beyond the intention or control of any of its participants. In every generation, the transmission of the blessing is not only problematic, but laden with mystery. The process of transmission into the next generation is not fully accomplished through human intentionality. Thus Isaac comes late to his blessing. Isaac, moreover, must bless according to the oracle of the womb which destines Jacob to be primary. And Jacob himself, in his old age, inscrutably crosses his hands (Gen. 48:14)!

I find these stories important models for our own intergenerational work. They affirm to us that the arrival of the blessing is well beyond our control. One cannot dictate the shape of faith to the next generation. Parents do indeed learn over and over that the outcome of faith in the next generation is often not according to our plans, or even according to our best guess. There is a freighted mystery between the generations which cannot be penetrated. Thus we are able to see that the blessing is given in odd ways. We may nonetheless celebrate that the blessing did survive, willy-nilly, into the next generation, even if carried by characters whom the family storyteller regards as unlikely or inappropriate.

NARRATIVES WHICH COMMAND

The material of intergenerational transmission is rich, varied, and inexplicable. We have thus far considered three very different models of continuity:

(1) The six texts of recital seek to *incorporate* into the story the new generation which still thinks of itself to be an outsider to the strange sacramental activity of the parenting generation.

(2) The pedagogy of saturation in Deuteronomy 6:4-9 seeks to provide a *coherent construal* of reality through ongoing interpretation.

(3) The bestowal of blessing in Genesis bespeaks *inscrutable mystery* and *irreversible outcome* that defy our best intentions.

The practice of *incorporation, construal,* and *mysterious, irreversible bestowal* seeks to bind the young to the promises and identity of faith. Thus talk about *liberation, memory,* and *blessing* focuses on the very substance of faith. On the whole, however, parents do not think in terms of such loaded or long-term categories. Anxiety about transmission is usually much more mundane and concrete. More likely, parents want their children inducted into a moral tradition, so that they do not bring hurt upon themselves or shame upon their family. As we will expect from Deuteronomy 6:4-9, the tradition of moral reflection into which Israel's young are inducted is a distinctly theonomous one. That is, ethical reflection concerns living in a world ordered according to the purposes of God.

The ethical tradition of the Old Testament is, however, not excessively pious or theological. I suggest that the moral nurture of our children as it is concretely practiced tends to be excessively idealistic when they are young, and excessively calculating when they are older, but both the idealism and the calculation miss the main claims of anything like a Yahwistic ethic. It is our habit to teach only our very young the radical moral dimension of our faith, because we know they are powerless to enact any of that radicality.[14] And as soon as our young are old enough to enact our moral vision, we induct them into a quite different ethical practice of calculating pragmatism. I suspect that traditionally, young women have been longer kept within the idealistic mode, but clearly that is because they were longer kept powerless to enact those claims in any significant way.

It is clear that in conventional nurture and education, young men (boys) are given a sort of "rite of passage" into the cynical world of conflict and competition, and away from any visionary radicality. This is in part accomplished through athletics, but dominant societal assumptions support such a move. By contrast, as Carol Gilligan has demonstrated, at the time when young men are being transposed away from radicalness into "realism," young women are intentionally nurtured into domestication (withdrawal), and tilted away from anything that smacks of ethical radicalness, or anything else radical that touches the real world. As women gain access to real power, conversely, they are brought more fully and quickly into a practice of calculating pragmatism.[15] That growing propensity, however, is antithetical to our more domesticating protectiveness.

The ethical tradition we may entrust to our young is a powerfully Yahwistic claim. At the center of this ethical tradition is a person, a purpose, a character, a will. The cruciality of this claim is not that God is a threat, so that obedience is done out of fear. It is rather that this dangerous character is one who intends communion with us, who has made us so that our lives remain dissatisfied until we arrive at communion for which our lives are constituted.[16] The Psalms are clear that Israel *desires* God (cf. Psalm

73:25), and our ethical tradition asserts that this desire is God's own work with us. That is, we desire God because God has created us with that insatiable desire for communion which is expressed as praise, prayer, and obedience. It is this communion which is the matrix of all true obedience, for obedience is an outgrowth of being loved and loving, of being cared for and valued, and responding in grateful commitment.

It is clear that the pursuit of communion and entry into communion requires discipline and skill. We speak glibly of "first communion," but the church has always known, albeit in formalistic ways, that "first communion" is an awesome event which requires preparation. I would not want, however, to consign "communion" to the Eucharist, for the intimacy of communion is personal, spontaneous, and pre-Eucharist, mediated by an adult community that itself practices communion. In the process of communion, the child learns that "I am an end and not a means," even as neighbors are ends and not means. Our desire for God is an end in itself, even as God's desire for us is an end in itself. Entry into communion entails a radical break with our tendency to instrumentalism. Communion with God has no instrumental value but is an end in and for itself. I suspect children can experience this only as our adult inclination toward them moves beyond the instrumentation of our agenda, so that our relation to our children becomes an end in itself.

While there is something innocent and child-like about the pursuit and reception of communion, such a process is not romantic, idealistic, or excessively pious. The overriding question of ethics rooted in communion is, What shall we do with the *desire* which God has ordained into our lives? We have tended to think such innocent communion as an end in itself pertains only to the very young. I submit that as our young grow older, one of two things happens. On the one hand, the desire for communion is displaced, so that God-given desire is transposed into a practice of greed, ambition, or lust, i.e., a desire for control, security, and possessions. Our God-given desire *is* practiced, but now in deep distortion and without reference to the God who gives it. One can see this displacement in a consumer society which is driven by misdirected desire for money, power, security, satiation, or gratification. Our conventional word for communion with that which does not and cannot commune is "idolatry." The young of the faith community, as they grow older, can be nurtured in a critical conversation about idolatry which is misdirected desire which may end in satiation, but never in joy.[17]

On the other hand, when misdirected desire becomes destructive (or embarrassing), the alternative response is the stifling of desire, the denial of yearning, and the reduction of life to more acceptable and "moral" enterprises. This is the more characteristic "church" response to desire, which reduces faith to pragmatic, socially acceptable behavior, perhaps legalism which requires denial of the very desire which makes us alive in the image of God.

Thus the nurture of communion into adulthood as the true practice of self-in-community is a primary work of ethics. As our young grow older, a sense of self with and alongside this God provides an alternative to the twin modes of destructiveness as self-indulgence and as self-denial. The practice of communion is not a "middle" way. It is rather a genuine third alternative that starts out with a distinct sense of self apropos a distinct God who craves us and who wants to be craved by us. The evangel is that a third way is given us which is an alternative to the primary pathologies of our time.

The availability of this God as the subject and partner of communion is not given in abstract or in vacuum. The God who is the subject and partner of communion is known primarily and fundamentally in the narratives of this community. God is not a being "out there," but a character in a textual drama to which we are witnesses and potentially participants. If we will commune with this God, then we must traffic incessantly in this narrative which God inhabits. (We need not discuss the "facticity" of these stories; it is enough to engage, as in any artistic enterprise, in the willing suspension of disbelief.)

The stories which are given to us in the Bible mediate to us a God who is a real "character," who has depth, density, intensity, and freedom, who works in and through the narratives with a richness of texture. The work of narrative makes two resistances possible. On the one hand, the narrative character of God resists the reduction of God to settled metaphysical categories. (This resistance reflects the old quarrel between biblical faith and the Hellenistic categories of much church theology.) This God is so free as to be capable of anger, duplicity, pettiness, but also capable of large, powerful, and generous acts. On the other hand, more contemporarily, the narrative character of God also resists reduction to a one-dimensional technological "explanation" which posits everything in a controllable system of outcomes. Indeed, it is the quality of surprise that most marks the character of God. And it is this quality of surprise that destabilizes every certitude onto which we hold, whether personal, theological, economic, or political.

Even the "great narrative" around which faith revolves regularly turns on specific moments of conversation and quite personal transactions, so that in our study of God we come down to what God did and said in a quite particular circumstance. Thus, the "story of the fall" (Gen. 3) comes down to what God said to this man and to this woman. The "great narrative" of the Exodus pivots on a series of conversations with Moses (and Aaron) which in turn yields conversations with Pharaoh. Much of the story is getting the conversation exactly right, making sure that the precise lines are known and reiterated in their proper cadences.

Because God lives in stories that permit a gamut of experience from fear, affront, and dismay to joy, surprise, and delight, it is clear that God lives on the lips of story-tellers. This point can hardly be overemphasized in a society that lacks the patience or density of imagination to tell and hear stories. This does not mean that the stories told about this God who wants and offers communion are always great "theological" stories or splendid ethical enactments. They are just family stories, belonging alongside the old stories treasured in the family about "Uncle Boots" and "Uncle Howard" and "Cousin Lizzie." While God may indeed be odd and "different," in the mode of narrative this God figures like others in the family as an active force, continually present and demanding attention.

If one listens to family stories, moreover, one is struck by their intense particularity. Such stories usually conclude with the central character uttering some outrageous one-liner which draws them, perhaps long since dead, back into the vitality of the family. The family is thereby gathered and energized in its belonging. To be a part of the family (as new in-laws discover), is to learn those concluding one-liners with great precision, so that very often the story need not be told in full, but only the one-liner recited.

The Bible is like that. The God of the Bible is often the one who is the speaker or subject of the narrative zinger. Belonging means to know and understand the freight of the one-liner, and therefore to engage the God who often utters the one-liner.

Now one may ask what this has to do with evangelism. Simply this: such narrative — narrative aimed at communion — is not just any old narrative, but it is good news. The good news is that our lives are centered on this character who dominates our imagination, who includes us as members of this story-telling, communion-practicing community quite unlike members of any other community. For starters, it leaves this community with a density of imagination, open and receptive, not trapped in either the power of acquisitiveness or in the throes of legalism. The center of existence is in the delight of the drama which puts life in a certain trajectory. I believe that ethics is fated to be coercive, unless the pool of narrative imagination forms the context of ethical insistence.

This communion-in-narrative of course issues in *commands*. For Israel and the church, ethics centers in the ten commands. Luther understood well the centrality of the decalogue in the practice of first communion, for the one with whom the church communes is the Lord of the commands. Finally it comes down to that, but it does not come down to that quickly or simply. It is important that the God who issues the commands is the same God who is present in such narrative playfulness.[18] There is no doubt that often the church has focused on the commands in a heavy-handed way, and has acted as though the commands are absolute and contextless, rather than given by the One endlessly present in narrative imagination.

Let me suggest an analogy. As we grow older, we discover that our parents "stood for something." They did not (most did not) stand on a mountain and give us a summary of their convictions on clay tablets. Over time, however, certain goals, values, and hopes have been voiced, repeatedly. When we reflect later, we may begin to sift out and even formulate, that of all the stuff "my dad" or "mother" said, these are the matters about which they cared the most. A wise parent makes sure that those "most cared about matters" are reinforced in many different ways. In the end, these matters may be noticed and remembered, even though the memory contains other distracting material, even matters that contradict the central matters. Sufficient reflection will often lead to an awareness of the "organizing imperatives" relentlessly insisted upon by parents.

This is of course only an analogy. I do not press it too far. I do suggest, however, that the ten commands turn out to be God's most "cared for matters." While there is no doubt tension and even contradiction between the narrative vitality of God and the singular authoritativeness of the commands, the remembering, assenting community finds it possible both to enjoy the narrative and to receive the commands, refusing to choose between the two.

Thus I propose that as our young are inducted into narrative delight about this unavoidable character, so our young may focus on the matters about which God cares the most. What God most cares about is love of God and love of neighbor. That is, God wants our desire for communion not to be distorted or misdirected. God wants neighbors, their lives, their bodies, their property, respected and treated as ends and not means. The commands are so simple; they invite to a very difficult alternative, eschewing both destructive self-indulgence at the expense of God and neighbor, and destructive self-denial which delights in neither God nor neighbor. It may only be late, as it often is with a remembered parent, that we discover that these seemingly innocuous and perfectly obvious statements are laden with revolutionary implications. Inducting our young into these matters "most cared about" by God could indeed rescue our young from the deathliness that comes with the terrible idolatries of our society.

The commands of God are endlessly restless and problematic. Too often the church has been willing to settle for the one-liner commands, without recognizing their density, complexity, or problematic quality. When the commands are taken in such a way, it is almost inevitable that they will be dismissed as irrelevant or consigned to small, privatized areas of our life. In fact, the matters about which our parents most cared continue to work on us in fresh ways. Very often we discover that their insistence, insight, and requirement touch parts of our emerging lives about which they themselves had no notion. Thus the "most cared about" matters continue to be generative, reaching well beyond their original scope.[19]

Mutatis mutandis, the ten commandments as God's "most cared about matters" continue to have ongoing, generative effectiveness.[20] Said another way, the commandments keep receiving and requiring interpretation and reinterpretation, as we discover they are the fount of an ongoing ethical tradition which has enormous moral and intellectual vitality.[21] The commandments endlessly insist upon reinterpretation. One can see this especially in the book of Deuteronomy which is a prime example of reinterpretation of the commands. One can, however, see the same activity in many places in the Bible and in the tradition of the church. Indeed, it is clear that the only other alternative to endless reinterpretation is that the commands will be dismissed as dead and irrelevant.

I cite only one case in point. The tenth commandment is "Thou shalt not covet."[22] In a child-like way, this may be a warning against envy and jealousy. But more poignantly, it may be understood as a comment upon systemic acquisitiveness. Now, with our growing awareness of the "rape of the earth," it is not unreasonable to see the command as a warning against the kind of greediness, expressed as policy or free-market ideology, as a curb on the destruction of the ecosystem of creation.

Our young need to know about and participate in the process of ethical generativity and vitality with the commands. My impression is that our young, e.g., an articulate high school student, a bright college sophomore or graduate student, often has not been helped to know that this ethical tradition is one that makes important claims in current political and economic practice. While such interpretation may go far afield from the initial statement, it is unthinkable that the God who has stated what is "most cared about," does not continue to care in sovereign ways amidst our own ethical complexity. As in every live family, the remembered character in the story continues to have a powerful say in the ongoing life of the family.

Along with the tradition of command, the Bible offers a second mode of ethical reflection pertinent to our young, namely the wisdom tradition, best known to us in the Book of Proverbs. This material is a collection of the best moral, intellectual reflections of the community.[23]

The wisdom teaching pertains especially to our subject because the instructional tone of the material is characteristically an adult addressing "my son." (We may take the formula in a less patriarchically-oriented society to include "my daughter.") Scholars are not able to decide if this is family teaching in which parents really do address children, or if it is a school in which the teacher addresses students in the role and guise of parent and child.[24] In either case, this textual tradition is the voice of the older generation addressing the younger generation, transmitting to it its trusted deposit of moral learning. There are some things this community has learned from experience, and the younger generation does not need to reinvent the wheel.

Knowledge, as every graduate student learns, is essentially fiduciary.[25] That is, what we are able to learn anew depends upon accepting as reliable much that has been learned before us, and we must trust the conclusions of our teachers. The new learning does not stand in isolation, but is situated and positioned within a community that already knows and trusts a great deal.[26] While this fact is obviously true in sociology or geology or music, it is equally true in the art and skill of living. The Book of Proverbs is a process of inculcating the young into a specific and certain angle of vision about the shape of moral freedom, moral possibility, and moral limit in the world. Israel asserts that a lot is already known!

The way in which the older generation speaks to the younger is crucial.[27] While there is some didacticism in these sapiential texts, on the whole the speech is "cool" and nonauthoritarian. Unlike the commands at Sinai, there is here no appeal to transcendant authority. Indeed, there is not even an imposition of the authority of parent or teacher. The only appeal is to the validity of experience and to the power and reliability of the observation. Clearly the adult speaker in the act of speech intends to speak as one with authority. But that authority is non-intrusive and non-invasive. It gives the listener a lot of room for negotiation, and invites the listener to come alongside in observation.

At the same time, it is clear that this mode of discourse is not neutral, so that we are given "technical" observation. There is an underlying moral conviction voiced here, of seeing immediate and concrete aspects of daily life in a larger horizon, and inviting the young to see that horizon as well.

The angle of vision assumed and urged in this teaching is that immediate experience is located in a larger moral coherence. Or put another way, "everything is related to everything," and the specificities of life make a whole.[28] There is no isolated act, and there is no act that can be undertaken with impunity as though to avoid its consequences or outcomes. Thus for example, the wisdom teachers through long observation have drawn conclusions about conduct in relation to sexuality (Prov. 7:10-27), work (10:4), words (10:17-18), money (11:24-25), and a host of other topics. Notice how practical the discussion is. Moreover, in each case, the teacher insists upon both the moral danger and the moral possibility present in the subject matter. There is no appeal to "God's will" or even to theological categories. Rather than speaking of "sin," this text characteristically speaks of "foolishness," i.e., the capacity for self-destruction.[29]

We may identify two scholarly constructs useful for this mode of nurture. First, Zimmerli has observed that wisdom teaching is "creation theology."[30] That is, it is a reflection upon the moral fabric of order which God has ordained into the world, which cannot be safely violated.[31] Second, Koch, followed by many others, has observed in this teaching an affirmation of "Deeds-Consequences," so that certain deeds have certain consequences, because life is ordered by God in that way.[32] The adult generation here invites the young to reflect upon the inscrutable ways in which consequences follow deeds. The future lies latent in how one acts.

This teaching is pertinent to our young who are often recruited into a deeply individualistic notion of technical reason which is inherently atheistic. It is easy, if one is affluent and well educated, to imagine that one can make choices in isolation, that one can make decisions for self without reference to neighbor. Even in our affluence, however, our young are learning that chemical dependence and sexual permissiveness are dangerous and no longer "safe." That same generation has yet to learn that acquisitiveness, greed, and indifference to neighbor, i.e., economic permissiveness, is also dangerous and no longer "safe." The reason for that cost, so this adult voice asserts, is because God has ordered the world so that acts are interrelated in the fabric of creation. This tradition of ethical reflection invites the young away from a supposed world of instrumental reason into a world where reason and communal fabric come together.

The teaching of this moral fabric is not sounded frontally in this teaching. It is rather voiced in playful and imaginative sayings that elusively connect seemingly unrelated matters, that draw analogies, that order and prioritize values, actions, and goods. These are the kinds of moral observations that tease, invite reflection, evoke imagination, and sketch out a world ordered beyond our control, in which our use of freedom matters enormously.

The Book of Proverbs is not the end of wisdom. In the wake of Proverbs comes the critical rage of Job and the weary resignation of Ecclesiastes.[33] As Roland Murphy has seen, these voices are not a rejection of wisdom, but a continuation and deepening of wisdom instruction.[34] In the end, wisdom comes to the anguish of theodicy which pushes beyond experience to rage, doubt, resignation, and doxology. The terrible question of theodicy is not alien to the faithful community. Indeed the question belongs precisely and principally to this community seeking communion. I suggest that it is urgent that our children know about the crisis of faith and theodicy before going to college to discover Kafka, Nietzsche, and Dostoievsky. Indeed, in the end, this tradition of ethical reflection is more honest and more restless than any alternative available in the mesmerizing world of modernity. Our young are offered here a richness of honesty that is not elsewhere offered.

In three modes, *narrative, command,* and *wisdom*, it is clear that ethical reflection belongs to the nurture of our young. It is evident that this large tradition, in its several forms, does indeed make bold conclusions and sets perimeters of a non-negotiable kind. This tradition is not finally bent toward relativism.

I should insist, however, that at least as important, perhaps more important, is the ongoing process of reflection and interpretation. Of course we do our young a disservice if we end in relativism. We do our young an equal disservice, however, if we suggest to them a settled moral tradition in which the absolutes are all in place without work to do. The Bible makes clear that the moral dimension of covenantal reality permits and requires an ongoing interpretive conversation. That conversation is demanding work. It is at the same time, however, a work of joy, for in the very conversation we find healing, and are led beyond where we have ever been. A tradition of cynical indifference, a tradition of instrumental reason, and a tradition of fixed absolutes have much in common.[35] They all resist the work of conversation. Because the central character in our narrative imagination is a generative character, this peculiar ethical tradition is unfinished and requires our work. It is one of the great evangelistic opportunities to include our young in this unfinished business. This conversation is at least to discern God's will which is as yet partly hidden. More likely, the work of the conversation is to press and persuade God in new ways. The great issues facing us, issues of bio-medical ethics, of economic equity, of use and abuse of the created order, all require fresh address. This tradition will fund those who have courage, freedom, and nerve to sustain that unfinished work.

TELLING A PAST/DREAMING A FUTURE

The task of evangelizing our young is enormously urgent. Much for the future depends upon it. I will cite two texts which hint at the risk and the possibility.

Psalm 78:5-8

Psalm 78 provides the best case known to me in the Bible for the evangelism of our own young. The community is enjoined to tell its young the "glorious deeds of YHWH" (v. 4), i.e., to let the young know that our life is grounded in awesome miracles. (The Psalm is exactly a recital of such miracles.) The Psalm gives five important reasons "that the next generation" might know "the miracles."

(1) They should set their hope (confidence) in God (v. 7). The purpose of the recital of miracles is to give the young a reliable point of reference in a God who works transformation. The recital

draws the future into God's transformative fidelity.

(2) Failure to tell the miracles, so we infer from the Psalm, will lead in one of two directions. It may lead to a falsely placed confidence (trust) in an idol or in self, an unworthy confidence; or it may lead to a lack of confidence, i.e., a practice of despair, which results in destructiveness of self or neighbor or both. The Psalm invites the young into a buoyancy rooted in the God who spreads a table in the wilderness (v. 19).

(3) They should remember "the works of God" (v. 7). If there is no telling, there will be forgetting. A community which does not tell its stories ends in amnesia. In a stupor of amnesia, a community may think there is only "now," and there is only "us." We know from too many examples of recent time that people with amnesia are enormously open to suggestion, blind obedience, and easy administration. These memories make one angular, odd, and incapable of assimilation. It is clear that consumerism depends upon amnesia, in which "products" are substituted for social reference points, and in time, such "consumer values" lead to a shameless kind of brutality. The Psalm intends that the young should have a heart richly peopled by an energizing past.

(4) They should "keep his commandments" (v. 7). The Psalm does not want little moral automatons which are busy keeping rules. I submit that "keep his commandments" here envisions people who are alive to moral urgency, who know that, in every circumstance, the love of God and love of neighbor are compelling, even if not simple issues. The Psalm guards against folk who are in a moral stupor of indifference and self-indulgence, and who do not discern that the human process is essentially a moral process.

It is intended that the children should not be among those "whose heart was not steadfast" (v. 8). The awkward negative contrasting the generations expresses a wish for a generation with a steadfast heart. The term "steadfast" (*kun*) means founded, situated, well-grounded. A parallel use is in Psalm 112:7-8. In that Psalm, the righteous, well-grounded person is one who is not consumed by anxiety, not put at risk by every threat and rumor and every piece of bad news (vv. 6-8). The "steady heart" is one which has staying power and continuity in all kinds of crises. One upshot of such a steady heart is the practice of generosity (Ps. 112:5, 9), contributing to the well-being of the community.

(5) They are not among those "whose spirit is not faithful to God" (Ps. 78:8). Again, with an awkward negative, the Psalm envisions a new generation of those whose core inclination (spirit) is to be unreservedly committed to this God of justice and righteousness, and not seduced into any other loyalty or practice.

This ambitious Psalm contends that explicit nurture will eventuate in a very particular kind of person who is capable of a special kind of presence in the world. This person, free of despair, moral indifference, and of amnesia, is one capable of and inclined toward steadfastness, both in communal practice and in relation to God. The Psalm insists that such a person is possible only in the context of nurture in a horizon of miracle.

This Psalm, which comments upon the nurture of children, has an eye on the future of the world. It aims to generate persons who can take responsibility for the future of the world. That future in the end will not be wrought through those who are technically competent, though technical competence is important. It will be wrought by those who have the capacity, resources, inclination, and courage to imagine a world differently. Evangelism of our young concerns not only the well-being of the family or survival of the church. It concerns the future of the world which depends in the end upon steadfastness and fidelity. Evangelism is a conversation which summons, evokes, and legitimates a next generation who will care for the world well beyond the dominant technologies so seductive and ideologies so powerful among us.

Joel 2:28-29 (cf. Acts 2:17-18)

As Psalm 78 joins the present to the past, so Joel 2 joins the present to the future. The poem of Joel 2 anticipates a terrible devastation (vv. 1-17), but then a glorious rehabilitation which is the generous, powerful, jealous work of God (vv. 18-32). In vv. 18-27, the poem promises well-being which culminates with a promise that God will be in the midst of Israel (v. 27). The formulation of v. 27 echoes the formulation of Exodus 6:2, 7:5, 20:1-3, and reiterates the fundamental claim of the first command, "There is no other." Even in its most futuristic projection, Israel's rhetoric stays rigorously close to the Exodus formulation into which the children are already inducted.

Verses 28-29 are a subset of this wondrous anticipation. As a final wave of God's blessing, "afterward" God will give God's spirit, i.e., God's creative power which can evoke a newness (cf. Isa. 32:15). These verses are bracketed in v. 28a and 29b by a reference to God's spirit. The work of the spirit thus is announced in a chiastic fashion. The spirit concerns:

a sons and daughters
   b old men
   b^1 young men
a^1 male and female slaves

The two pairs together signify all parts of the community. What interests us is the "sons and daughters," and "young men." The terms are not quite symmetrical, because "sons and daughters" is parallel to "old men," thus lacking "young women" in the second pair. It is anticipated that the "sons and daughters, young men" will be swept up in the spirit and will "prophesy and see visions." The young in this faithful congregation will be energized, liberated, and authorized to envision a future and to imagine alternatives that are not grounded in present tense realities.

On the one hand, this work is wrought only because of God's inscrutable gift of the spirit. On the other hand, such "futuring" is possible because this community has been disciplined in readiness over a long period of time, fasting (v. 15), praying (v. 17), being unafraid (vv. 21-22) and confessing (v. 27). The poem is a clear assertion of that nurture the of the children is in order that the community may faithfully trust God into the future, and be able to conjure the future God intends. We may conclude that a community not visited by the spirit will be unable to host the future and will be consigned to an endless present tense (cf. Eccl. 1:7-10). Thus nurture of a day-to-day kind concerns precisely an openness to the newness that God is yet to work.

It is not unimportant that this is the poem that Luke-Acts places at the very beginning of the story of the church (Acts 2:17-21). The church is the community that is intruded upon by the spirit of God, and is lead out beyond the present to God's future. In the preaching of Peter, this empowerment for the future is linked to the power of God to work "deeds of power, wonders, and signs" culminating in the resurrection. The outcome is that "death could not hold him" (v. 24). Thus the spirit leads to the discernment and reception of God's power for new life, thereby refusing to submit to the power of death. This portrayal of the church as futuring to God's new life is uncommonly important in a society that is increasingly in love with death, fascinated by it, and courting it at every turn.[36] In a flatly technological society, it is of great moment to raise up a community of boys and girls with vision, who anticipate the gift of life.

Psalm 78 and Joel 2 form a poignant dialectic in two regards. First, they respectively concern a community grounded in the past and open to the future. Both resist an excessive commitment to present tense status quo. Second, they form a contrast. Whereas Psalm 78 speaks negatively about a community of the young not inducted, Joel 2 ponders a community fully prepared, open, and visited. The evangelism of boys and girls in this narratively shaped reality is a project of very large, very long-term importance.

A FRAGILE FIDELITY

I conclude with three texts that have informed me as I have pondered this conversation of nurture and discipline.

Psalm 103:13-14

It is striking that when the Psalmist speaks about God's gentleness toward God's people, the image is that of a father. (In a less partriarchal society, the image might well have been a mother.) God is like a father in two ways. First, like a father who has compassion. The term compassion (*riham*), as Phyllis Trible has shown, refers to womb-like mother love.[37] That is, the father here is "mother-like," in being completely concerned for the child, willing to care in inordinate ways and to stand in utter solidarity. Second, God is like a father who remembers "how we were made . . . that we are dust." The term "how we are made" (*yetser*) looks back to Genesis 2:7.[38] God is like a father who remembers where we came from, how we are born, of what we are made, and how utterly fragile and precarious we are.

The poem appeals to a community of parents which remembers the precious fragility of the child and holds no expectation that is beyond the capability of the child. This affirmation is easy enough with a very young child. This community of fathers and mothers, however, continues in that parental awareness later on, when the child no longer remembers fragility, when the child-become-adult pretends otherwise. Human life is deeply and endlessly at risk. The parents know this. While they cannot shield the child from that risk, they are present to the vulnerability of the child, honoring, caring, forgiving. It is in that matrix of unending compassion that these children are nurtured. They learn in the process that all of creation, framed from dust, is at risk, and needs gentle care commensurate with its vulnerability.

Luke 10:21-24

This odd text does not directly refer to parents and children, but is intensely Christological. I cite it in connection with our theme for two reasons. It refers to "infants" (v. 21) and to "disciples" (v. 23). The two terms "infants" and "disciples" concern those novices in faith who are exceedingly vulnerable, but capable of being taught and formed for trustful obedience.

It is likely that this statement of Jesus combines two independent sayings. In the first, (vv. 21-22), a contrast is made between the wise and intelligent for whom "these things" are *hidden* and "infants" to whom "these things" are *revealed*. The things revealed concern the relation of the father to the son, i.e., the claim that the power and will of the creator God is evident in the person of Jesus. The reference to "infant" is not to be taken literally, but refers to those whom the world regards as weak and insignificant. The powerful truth of reality, so this faith asserts, is more likely to be given to the little ones who are not so trapped in the wisdom and power of this age.

In the second saying (vv. 23-24), it is recognized that the disciples are permitted to see and hear what the powerful (kings and prophets) have not seen and heard. That is, vulnerability is a prerequisite to receive this gift of discernment and faith.

The two sayings together suggest that in the evangelism of its young, the church must not too readily imitate the world's linkage of power and knowledge. The discipling process is the induction of our young into this odd world where foolishness is wisdom and weakness is power (1 Cor. 1:18-25). The strange juxtaposition of these two sayings indicates that the dominant categories of the world will not hold. While the church wants its young to face the reality of the world in adult-like ways, at the same time it wants its adults to engage in child-like innocence and vulnerability, for the important turns in reality happen because of vulnerability. Such evangelical nurture must guard against a cynical world-wiseness as our young grow older, for self-possession in the end defeats miracle and precludes communion. This statement of Jesus affirms that an alternative in the world is possible which is not excessively wise or strong, but is fixed upon the mystery of the cross wherein God's ultimate power is disclosed. The power of the cross becomes the decisive element in "infants" who are "disciples."

Luke 1:16-17

The speech of the angel to Zechariah concerns this coming baby John. In vv. 16-17, John's anticipated work is governed by the double use of the verb, "turn." It is anticipated that John will cause a great conversion. First, he will convert many of the people of Israel who had fallen away. Second, and for our purposes more importantly, he will turn the hearts of parents to their children. It is astonishing that the text quotes Malachi 4:6 (Heb. 2:24), but does not continue the second half of Malachi's parallelism, but instead creates a new parallelism, "the disobedient to the wisdom of the righteous."

As Luke renders Malachi, the second line may precisely parallel the first line, so that "the disobedient" may be parents and the "wisdom of the righteous" may be that of the children. In any case, it is telling that in this version of Malachi's promise, it is the parents who are to turn to the children, not the children who must conform to the parents. If the fundamental disorder of the world is to be overcome, true conversion is that the parents should attend to their children in their innocence, their need, and especially their vulnerability, perhaps to honor it, perhaps to share in it.[39]

The outcome of such turning is "to make ready a people prepared." In context of the birth narratives, this means a people prepared for the coming of the messiah. More broadly, it is to make ready a people prepared for God's new ordering of reality. The nurture and evangelism of our children is that they may be ready for the cost and joy of the world ordered in new ways that seem odd to us. For us to turn for our children means dramatic disengagement from the despair, amnesia, and acquisitiveness that so mark our common consciousness (cf. Luke 3:10-14). This process of evangelism is not a domestic, institutional matter. It concerns large issues of the promise of God for the life of the world. In these words of anticipation, the well-being of the children depends upon the turning of the parents. "Turning" by parents to children means that it is parents who stand most in need of conversion. When parents "turn," the children will believe.

The present crisis of evangelism is in a great measure because the community of the church has not persuaded our own young of the power or validity of the gospel. I suspect that has happened because adults have been inarticulate within the family of faith about our faith. I imagine that a reason for inarticulateness is that the scandal of faith has become increasingly unpalatable for adults who crave easy accommodation between faith and culture. In the context of such an easy accommodation, the Christian faith is trimmed of all its radicalness, until there is very little about which to be articulate, and that very little has most often been boiled down to privatized legalism.

With the collapse of communist political and economic systems in Eastern Europe (and many think the collapse of Marxism as an intellectual option), on the surface we seem to be left with only free-market ideology among faith options. While this situation has evoked uncritical jubilation, it should be clear that free-market ideology is no adequate framework on which to build a viable human community. At best it is an ideology attractive to the productive self-sufficient; that ideology, however, is a very thin and inadequate place in which to stand. If the church abdicates with its young, they will inevitably grow up in our society as heirs to free-market ideology with its incredibly dehumanizing intention.

The challenge of evangelism in this regard is whether the

church can articulate a coherent way in the world that is in sore tension with the dominant ideology of the free market, whether we adults can bring our minds and hearts to that work, and whether we dare be so odd with our own young. If the gospel is a compelling force with us, the kids will catch on. If we present faith as only a romantic gift for the very young but not pertinent to "real life," the kids will notice that as well.

The requirement for us, as for our children, is that the Christian gospel should be voiced and heard as:

- intellectually credible in an unreflective society;
- politically critical and constructive in a cynical community;
- morally dense and freighted in a self-indulgent society;
- artistically satisfying in a society overwhelmed by religious kitsch; and
- pastorally attentive in a society of easy but fake answers.

No wonder we have a "scandal" on our hands! In time to come, the children may ask about the meaning of our faithful signs; or they may notice only our faint-heartedness. In their embarrassment for us, they may keep quiet and not ask anything. Our adult work is to struggle enough with faith to mediate its "news" to our precious, treasured off-spring. Without the news, we erode to death, we and our children.

CONCLUSION

Evangelism is no safe church activity that will sustain a conventional church, nor a routine enterprise that will support a societal status quo. Evangelism as here understood is an activity of *transformed consciousness* that results in an altered perception of world, neighbor, and self, and an authorization to live differently in that world. The news that God has triumphed means that a transformed life, i.e., one changed by the hearing of the news, works to bring more and more of life, personal and public, under the rule of this world-transforming, slave-liberating, covenant-making, promise-keeping, justice-commanding God.

The drama of evangelism is no once-for-all event, but it is a narrative that moves, repeatedly, through the sequence of *victory — proclamation — appropriation*. The Church as an evangelizing community is endlessly engaged itself in reenacting and appropriating this drama, and finding itself reincorporated into this dangerous alternative world. At the heart of this evangelical drama is a claim, the reality of which is hidden from us in ways that defy our technical capacity for certitude. At base, biblical faith is the assertion that God has overcome all that threatens to cheapen, enslave, or fragment our common life. Because the power of death is so resilient, this triumph of God is endlessly reiterated, reenacted, and replicated in new formats and venues. As a result of that always new victory, we are left to do our most imaginative proclamation and our most courageous appropriation.

The drama of hearing, responding, and appropriating is no one-dimensional generalization. Rather, the appropriation of the news well proclaimed is always concrete, particular, and subversive. In a culture-bound church such as most of the U.S. church is, our preferred strategy for evangelism is to invite people in, with the winking assurance that "everything" can remain the same.

Our study of this drama leads to the conclusion that nothing can remain the same, as it did not in the Bible itself. I imagine that a main issue for the U.S. church in thinking about evangelism is to recover the nerve (courage and freedom) to say unambiguously that embrace of the news is pervasively transformative.

We have, in this study, reflected upon this transformative reality in terms of three constituencies:

- No more business as usual for outsiders who have become insiders. Thus Joshua has in mind that if one "chooses Yahweh," one also chooses a covenantal ethic, and ceases the "Canaanite practices" of anti-neighbor living.
- No more business as usual for insiders who are freshly reincorporated into the scroll-oriented, boothing process of faith. Insiders are reinvited into the passions of covenant and become children of a command that touches all parts of life.
- No more business as usual even for our young, who otherwise think only of growing up benignly, with all the privileges and gifts of dominant culture.

The church of course does not want to be excessively radical, disruptive, or subversive. No, of course not. Nor do I. The warrant and urgency for "no more business as usual" is located not in the fact that one is a sore-head or a hot-head, or even because the claim is in the Bible (perhaps a good enough reason). No. The urgency of this counter-claim of transformation is rather that there is mediated here the possibility of life that is not available to "Canaanite" outsiders, or to jaded insiders, or to undecided young persons. In the end, the God who gains a victory over chaos for the sake of the world, over death for the sake of life, over injustice for the sake of *shalom*, is the one for whom we desperately and unwittingly yearn. This is not an ecclesial matter, and evangelism is not in the end an ecclesial agenda. It is rather an offer that we might be on the receiving end of "all things new." We are invited by this old text, when well said and well dramatized, to *retell* our life.[1] The telling is an evangelical act. We are potentially the tellers, the hearers, and the livers. Without such news, we languish away from the God of life into despair. But we need not, because there are texts enough even for newness.

NOTES

Chapter 1: Evangelism in Three Unfinished Scenes

1. On the move from then and there to here and now, see Walter Brueggemann, *Israel's Praise: Doxology Against Idolatry and Ideology* (Philadelphia: Fortress Press, 1988), 29-38, and Garrett Green, *Imagining God: Theology and the Religious Imagination* (San Francisco: Harper and Row, 1989), 62-74.

2. The reason no single shape can be normative is that every shaping is "theory laden," i.e., not objective. See Richard Harvey Brown, *Society as Text: Essays on Rhetoric, Reason, and Reality* (Chicago: University of Chicago Press, 1987), 68 and *passim*.

3. Paul Hanson, *The Dawn of the Apocalyptic* (Philadelphia: Fortress Press, 1975), has shown the decisive connection between the oldest myths and the later apocalyptic texts.

4. On the resilient, unconquered power of evil, see Jon D. Levenson, *Creation and the Persistence of Evil* (San Francisco: Harper and Row, 1988).

5. See Johann Christiaan Beker, *Paul the Apostle: The Triumph of God in Life and Thought* (Philadelphia: Fortress Press, 1980).

6. Norman K. Gottwald, *The Tribes of Yahweh* (Maryknoll, NY: Orbis Books, 1979), has shown most comprehensively that the Exodus-Sinai crisis in Israel was a social revolution concerning modes of social relationships. He has urged that the Exodus-Conquest was a liberation from modes of domination and an exercise in egalitarian social relationships.

7. See Walter Brueggemann, "The Commandments and Liberated, Liberating Bonding," *Journal for Preachers* 102 (Lent, 1987), 15-24, re-

printed in *Interpretation and Obedience: From Faithful Reading to Faithful Living* (Minneapolis: Fortress Press, 1991), 145-58.

8. On the way in which Luke-Acts reiterates the dramatic propensities of Deuteronomy, see John Drury, *Tradition and Design in Luke's Gospel* (Atlanta: John Knox Press, 1976), 138-71, and C. F. Evans, "The Central Section of St. Luke's Gospel," *Studies in the Gospels: Essays in Honor of R. H. Lightfoot*, ed. D. E. Nineham (Oxford: Blackwell, 1955), 37-53. See the recent recasting of the argument by David Moessner, "Luke 9:1-50: Luke's Preview of the Journey of the Prophet Like Moses of Deuteronomy," *Journal of Biblical Literature* 102 (1983), 575-605, and *Lord of the Banquet* (Minneapolis: Fortress Press, 1989).

9. On the epistemological crisis of evangelical faith, see Sharon D. Welch, *Communities of Resistance and Solidarity* (Maryknoll, NY: Orbis Books, 1985), 9-14 and *passim*.

10. On the destructive seduction of commodities, see Abraham Heschel, *Who is Man?* (Stanford: Stanford University Press, 1965), 83-87 and *passim*, and Brown, *Society as Text: Essays on Rhetoric, Reason and Reality* (Chicago: University of Chicago Press, 1987), 64-79.

11. By focusing on this issue I do not risk reductionism, because I am aware that there is a complex web of idolatries and oppressions which play upon each other; I intend my analysis to allude to all of these elements of the current crisis.

12. On the public aspect of forgiveness, see Carter Heyward et al. and the Amanecida Collective, *Revolutionary Forgiveness: Feminist Reflections on Nicaragua* (Maryknoll, NY: Orbis Books, 1987).

13. On the phrase, see Krister Stendahl, "The Apostle Paul and the Introspective Conscience of the West," *Paul Among Jews and Gentiles and Other Essays* (Philadelphia: Fortress Press, 1976), 78-96.

14. Jesus' parable in Mark 4:1-20 fully acknowledged this inevitable reality.

15. On the lean intent of proclamation of the gospel, see the stunning narrative of Vincent J. Donovan, *Christianity Rediscovered* (Maryknoll, NY: Orbis Books, 1982).

16. Peter Berger and Thomas Luckman, *The Social Construction of Reality* (Anchor Books; Garden City, NY: Doubleday, 1967), 156-57, use the nice phrase "switches worlds."

Chapter 2: Outsiders Become Insiders

1. See Dennis McCarthy, "An Installation Genre?" *Journal of Biblical Literature* 90 (March, 1971), 31-41.

2. On this pivotal chapter, see William T. Koopmans, *Joshua 24 as Poetic Narrative* (JSOT Supp. 93; Sheffield: Sheffield Academic Press, 1991).

3. Albrecht Alt, "Die Wallfahrt von Sichem nach Bethel," *Kleine Schriften zur Geschichte des Volkes Israel I* (Munich: C. H. Beck Verlagsbuch-handlung, 1953), 79-88.

4. The connection of these texts to baptismal practice has been argued effectively by Philip Carrington, *The Primitive Christian Catechism: A Study in the Epistles* (Cambridge: Cambridge University Press, 1940).

5. For the phrase, see Peter L. Berger and Thomas Luckmann, 156-57.

6. Patrick D. Miller, Jr., "The Human Sabbath: A Study in Deutero-nomic Theology," *The Princeton Seminary Bulletin* 6/2 (1985), 81-97.

Chapter 3: Forgetters Made Rememberers

1. See the programmatic essay of James A. Sanders, "Torah and Christ," *Interpretation* 29 (October, 1975), 372-90.

2. David Tracy, *The Analogical Imagination: Christian Theology and the Culture of Pluralism* (New York: Crossroad, 1981), has reflected on how the "classic" requires ongoing interpretation. See his comments on the timelessness and timeliness of a classic, a dialectic that depends on interpretation (p. 102).

3. The term "lack nothing" (*haser*) is the same term as in the familiar line of Ps. 23:1: "The Lord is my shepherd, I shall not *want*." The claim of the Psalm is that the generosity of God results in abundance, completely without lack or scarcity. What appears to be a religious affirmation in the Psalm, in this sermon of Moses receives quite concrete content.

4. Gustavo Gutiérrez, *We Drink From Our Own Wells: The Spiritual Journey of a People* (Maryknoll, NY: Orbis Books, 1984), has taken the metaphor of water from wells, a phrase from Bernard of Clairvaux, to speak of the sources of spirituality. Whereas Gutiérrez speaks of wells which have deep resources, Jeremiah uses the same metaphor negatively concerning a people which has no resources for life.

5. For a fresh and largely negative assessment of the circumstance of the exiles in Babylon, see Daniel L. Smith, *The Religion of the Landless: The Social Context of the Babylonian Exile* (Bloomington: MyerStone Books, 1989).

6. It is this situation of the U.S. church that has evoked the radical and much disputed metaphor and argument of Stanley Hauerwas and

William H. Willimon, *Resident Aliens: Life in the Christian Colony* (Nashville: Abingdon Press, 1989).

Chapter 4: Beloved Children Become Belief-ful Adults

1. The title of this chapter is a paraphrase from Alfred North Whitehead, *The Aims of Education and Other Essays* (London: Williams and Norgate, 1932), 43. Whitehead asserts of education: "Its business is to convert the knowledge of a boy into the power of a man." In like manner, the purpose of nurture is to convert beloved children into adults capable of serious faith.

2. The children of believers may indeed be candidates for the program of Horace Bushnell, i.e., children so nurtured in faith that they never know themselves as other than persons of faith.

3. In such a context, there is no "once and for all" event or experience of conversion. Even the benign practice of confirmation has proceeded programmatically and liturgically as if this were "once for all" into adult faith. Obviously this has little resonance with the reality of growing into adulthood.

4. That numbed withdrawal has been especially important in the work of Robert Jay Lifton. Indeed, he has suggested that such a numbing occurs because of a "symbol gap," i.e., a situation in which there is a lack of symbols adequate for the depth and danger of experience. Without an adequate symbol, the available experience cannot be experienced and is in fact refused.

5. See Urie Bronfenbrenner, "Who Needs Parent Education?" *Teachers College Record* 79 (1978), 773-74, and Nel Noddings, *Caring: A Feminine Approach to Ethics and Moral Education* (Berkeley: University of California Press, 1984), 59-78. Bronfenbrenner proposes that such care in the end produces "competence" and a capacity for "response-ability."

6. On these texts, see Walter Brueggemann, *The Creative Word: Canon as a Model for Biblical Education* (Philadelphia: Fortress Press, 1982), 14-39.

7. J. A. Soggin, "Kultaetiologische Sagen und Kateches im AT," *Vetus Testamentum* 10 (1960), 341-47, has suggested that these questions and responses constitute something like a catechism. The important difference from our conventional catechisms, however, is that the child asks and the adult answers.

8. On the abiding power of such wonders to continue to destabilize, see Walter Brueggemann, *Abiding Astonishment: Psalms, Modernity, and the*

Making of History (Literary Currents in Biblical Interpretation; Louisville: Westminster/John Knox Press, 1991).

9. Michael Fishbane, "Deuteronomy 6:20-25/Teaching and Transmission," *Text and Texture: Close Readings of Selected Biblical Texts* (New York, Schocken Books, 1979), 79-83.

10. The term is used by Fishbane, "Deuteronomy 6:20-25," 82, with reference to the important discussion of Eugen Rosenstock-Huessy, *Speech and Reality* (Norwich, Vermont: Argo Books Inc., 1970), 33.

11. On this crucial text, see the discussion of Patrick D. Miller, *Deuteronomy* (Interpretation; Louisville: Westminster/John Knox Press, 1990), 97-106, his reference to the studies of J. G. Janzen and S. Dean McBride, and Patrick D. Miller, "The Most Important Word: The Yoke of the Kingdom," *Iliff Review* 41 (1984), 17-30.

12. On the power of blessing entrusted to Israel, see Hans Walter Wolff, "The Kerygma of Yahwist," *Interpretation* 20 (1966), 131-58, reprinted in *The Vitality of Old Testament Traditions*, by Walter Brueggemann and Hans Walter Wolff (Atlanta: John Knox Press, 1982), 41-66, and Claus Westermann, "The Way of the Promise through the Old Testament," *The Old Testament and Christian Faith*, edited by Bernhard W. Anderson (New York: Harper and Row, 1963), 200-224.

13. The narrative of Hagar is a crucial element and a paradigmatic case of the struggle for the blessing among ancestors. On the internal textuality of the Hagar narrative, see Phyllis Trible, *Texts of Terror: Literary-Feminist Readings of Biblical Narratives* (Overtures; Philadelphia: Fortress Press, 1984), 9-35, and on the historical and narrative antecedents of the biblical account, see Jo Ann Hackett, "Rehabilitating Hagar: Fragments of an Epic Pattern," *Gender Difference in Ancient Israel*, edited by Peggy L. Day (Minneapolis: Fortress Press, 1989), 12-27.

14. I am grateful to Ernest Marvin, pastor of St. Columba United Church in Cambridge, England for this shrewd assessment of the ways in which radicality in faith has a negative correlation to the acquisition of effective social power.

15. See Carol Gilligan, et al., *Making Connections: The Relational Worlds of Adolescent Girls at Emma Willard School* (Cambridge: Harvard University Press, 1990), and *Women, Girls and Psychotherapy: Reframing Resistance*, edited by C. Gilligan, A. Rogers, and D. Talisman (New York: Haworth Press, 1991).

16. I intend, of course, to allude to Augustine's well-known aphorism. That aphorism, however, is not to be trivialized into a pious over-simplification. It is rather an honest and sophisticated awareness of the ways in which our lives are driven by desire. Rupert Hoare has called my attention to the shrewd psychological analysis of Adam Smith in *Wealth of Nations*,

as he understood how a market economy depends upon the nurture of desire. Freud's programmatic understanding of culture, moreover, concerns the necessary enactment and necessary renunciation of desire.

17. Luther's exposition of the first two commandments continues to be the most powerful exposition of the crisis of idolatry we have. See Pablo Richard, et al., *The Idols of Death and the God of Life* (Maryknoll, NY: Orbis Books, 1983). On the absence of joy in the practice of idolatry, see Psalm 51:8, 12, which recognizes that a violation of God leads to the departure of joy which cannot be generated by an alternative to the true God. The teaching is a hard one, but one whose exposition is crucial in a consumer economy.

18. The relation between narrative and law is a very old and vexing problem for biblical scholarship. While there are enormously difficult critical questions concerning the topic, we might do better to consider the ways in which imperatives do indeed arise from the storytelling of serious communities of interpretation. The commands lose power and authority when they are no longer embedded in an active practice of narrative recital.

19. It is evident in the Old Testament community of narrative and command that there was no "strict constructionism" about the law of Moses. The hermeneutical vitality reflected in the book of Deuteronomy makes unmistakable that the commands of Moses insisted upon endless interpretation and recontextualization. It is clear that "strict constructionism," either with reference to the Supreme Court of the U.S., or with reference to religiously orthodox morality is a partisan ideological device and not a theory of law.

20. See the imaginative way in which Walter Harrelson, *The Ten Commandments and Human Rights* (Overtures; Philadelphia: Fortress Press, 1980), has shown how the ten commandments continue to be pertinent and generative for all kinds of new ethical issues and contexts.

21. See my own discussion of this moral and intellectual vitality in "The Commandments and Liberated, Liberated Bonding," *op cit.*

22. See my exposition of this command in *Finally Comes the Poet: Daring Speech for Proclamation* (Minneapolis: Fortress Press, 1989), 99-110.

23. For an introduction into this material, see Gerhard von Rad, *Wisdom in Israel* (Nashville: Abingdon Press, 1972), and James L. Crenshaw, *Old Testament Wisdom: An Introduction* (Atlanta: John Knox Press, 1981).

24. See Hans Walter Wolff, *Anthropology of the Old Testament* (Philadelphia: Fortress Press, 1974), 178-84. On the several contexts for wisdom instruction, see several articles in *The Sage in Israel and the Ancient Near East*, edited by John G. Gammie and Leo G. Perdue (Winona Lake:

Eisenbrauns, 1990), specifically on the court (R. N. Whybray, 133-39), the family and tribe (Carol R. Fontaine, 155-64), and the school and temple (Andre Lemaire, 165-81).

25. On the fiduciary character of knowledge, see Michael Polanyi, *Personal Knowledge: Towards a Post-Critical Philosophy* (Chicago: University of Chicago Press, 1958).

26. The normative statement of this matter is by Thomas S. Kuhn, *The Structure of the Scientific Revolutions* (Chicago: University of Chicago Press, 1970).

27. Gerhard von Rad, *Wisdom in Israel*, 24-50, and wisdom studies generally have paid great attention to the ways in which wisdom is expressed and transmitted. James Crenshaw has provided several important studies on this issue. See especially "Education in Ancient Israel," *Journal of Biblical Literature* 104 (1985), 601-15, "Wisdom and Authority: Sapiential Rhetoric and Its Warrants," *Supplements to Vetus Testamentum* 32 (1981), 10-29.

28. I am indebted to Sara Little for this particular phrasing. I take the affirmation to be a counter to the seduction of technical reason which believes it can dissolve reality into discrete units. The affirmation about connectedness is at the heart of wisdom instruction and is reflected in a theological understanding of creation as a connected system. See Hans Heinrich Schmid, *Gerechtigkeit als Weltordnung* (BHT 40, Tübingen: Mohr/Siebeck, 1968), and "Creation, Righteousness, and Salvation: 'Creation Theology' as the Broad Horizon of Biblical Theology," *Creation in the Old Testament*, edited by Bernhard W. Anderson (Philadelphia: Fortress Press, 1984), 102-17.

29. Von Rad, *Wisdom in Israel*, 65, concludes, "Folly is practical atheism." On p. 83, he refers to the fool as a "disorderly" man. More broadly on "folly," see Barbara W. Tuchman, *The March of Folly from Troy to Vietnam* (New York: Ballantine Books, 1984).

30. Walther Zimmerli, "The Place and Limit of the Wisdom in the Framework of the Old Testament Theology," *Scottish Journal of Theology* 17 (1964), 146-58, and specifically p. 148.

31. This is a conclusion that follows from the arguments of Schmid, on which see n. 28 above. Schmid's perspective, of course has not gone unchallenged; see Horst Dietrich Preuss, *Theologie des Alten Testaments I* (Stuttgart: W. Kohlhammer, 1919), 259-74.

32. The classic statement is that of Klaus Koch, "Is there a Doctrine of Retribution in the Old Testament?" in *Theodicy in the Old Testament*, edited by James L. Crenshaw (Philadelphia: Fortress Press, 1983), 57-87; see the critique of Patrick D. Miller, *Sin and Judgment in the Prophets* (Chico, CA: Scholars Press, 1982), 121-39.

33. Over time, James Crenshaw has written extensively and most helpfully on the ways in which these literary pieces relate to the crisis of theodicy in ancient Israel. In his recent commentary, *Ecclesiastes* (OTL, Philadelphia: Westminster Press, 1987), 12-13, an extensive part of Crenshaw's impressive bibliography on the subject is provided.

34. Roland E. Murphy, "Qoheleth's 'Quarrel' with the Fathers," *From Faith to Faith: Essays in Honor of Donald G. Miller on his Seventieth Birthday*, edited by Dikran Y. Hadidian (Pittsburgh: Pickwick Press, 1979), 235-45.

35. On the quite distinct locations of rival ethical traditions, see Alasdair C. MacIntyre, *Whose Justice? Which Rationality?* (Notre Dame: University of Notre Dame Press, 1989), and *Three Rival Versions of Moral Enquiry: Encyclopedia, Genealogy & Tradition* (Notre Dame: University of Notre Dame Press, 1990).

36. On "love of death," see Isaiah 28:15, 18. More broadly, see Robert Jay Lifton, *The Broken Connection: On Death and the Continuity of Life* (New York: Basic Books, 1979), and his many related studies, and in a very different way, Ernest Becker, *The Denial of Death* (New York: Free Press, 1973), and Erich Fromm, *Escape From Freedom* (New York: Rinehart and Co., 1941).

37. Phyllis Trible, *God and the Rhetoric of Sexuality* (Overtures, Philadelphia: Fortress Press, 1978), 31-71.

38. See Walter Brueggemann, "Remember, You are Dust," *Journal for Preachers* 14/2 (Lent, 1991), 3-10.

39. On this turn toward the children, see Alice Miller, *Thou Shalt Not be Aware: Society's Betrayal of the Child* (New York: New American Library, 1986).

Conclusion

1. On the theme of "retelling," see the suggestive and programmatic work of Roy Schafer, *Retelling a Life; Narrative and Dialogue in Psychoanalysis* (New York: Basic Books, 1992).